Five-Star Trails

Spokane

30 Spectacular Hikes in the Inland Northwest

SETH MARLIN

MENASHA RIDGE PRESS
Your Guide to the Outdoors Since 1982

Five-Star Trails: Spokane

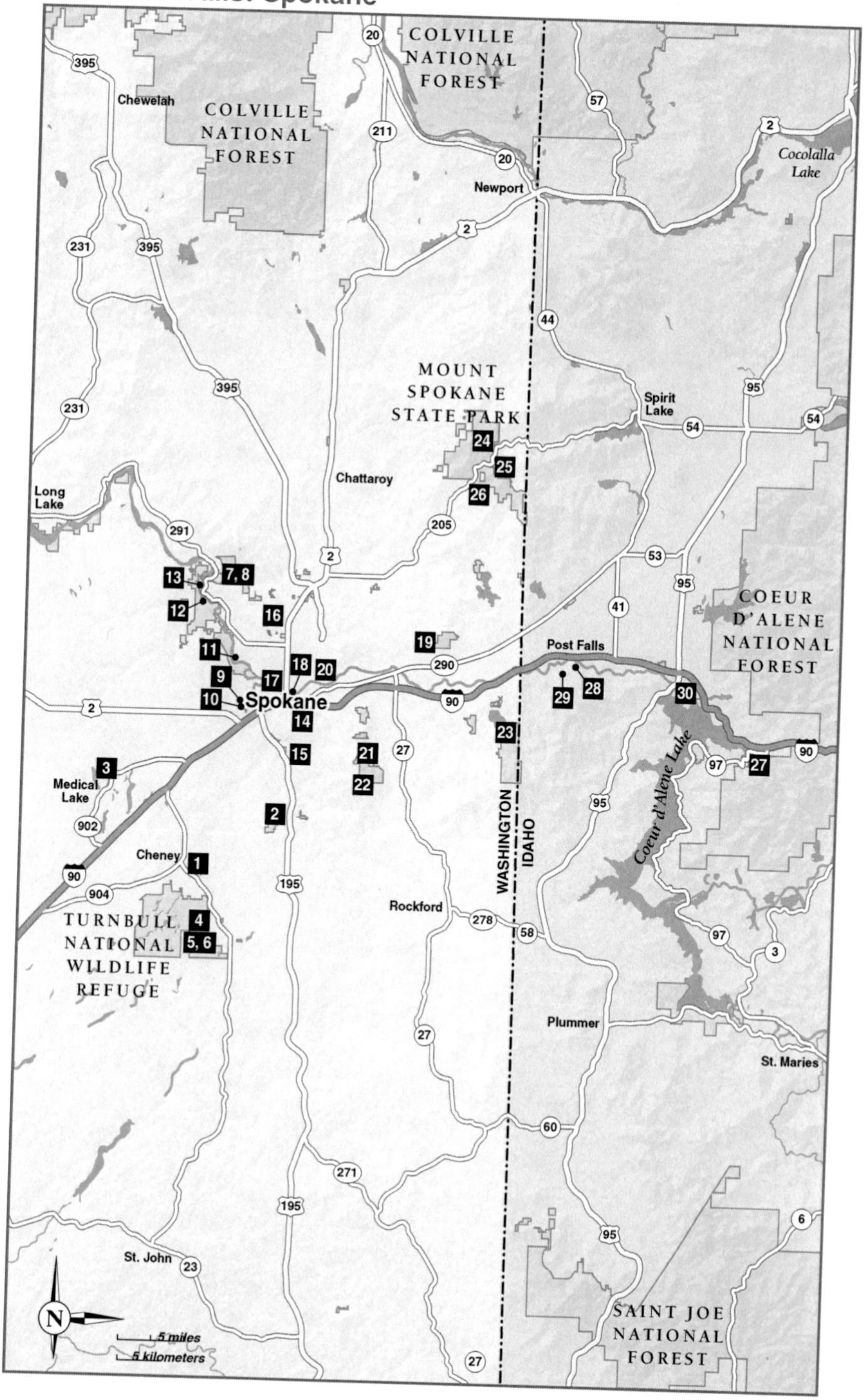

COLVILLE NATIONAL FOREST

COLVILLE NATIONAL FOREST

Chewelah

Cocolalla Lake

Newport

MOUNT SPOKANE STATE PARK

Chattaroy

Spirit Lake

Long Lake

Post Falls

COEUR D'ALENE NATIONAL FOREST

Spokane

Coeur d'Alene Lake

Medical Lake

Cheney

WASHINGTON

IDAHO

Rockford

Plummer

TURNBULL NATIONAL WILDLIFE REFUGE

St. Maries

St. John

SAINT JOE NATIONAL FOREST

N

5 miles

5 kilometers

Overview Map Key

Five-Star Trails: Spokane

Copyright © 2020 by Seth Marlin
All rights reserved

Published by Menasha Ridge Press
Distributed by Publishers Group West
First edition, first printing

Project editor: Amber Kaye Henderson
Cover design and cartography: Scott McGrew
Text design: Annie Long
Photos: Seth Marlin except as noted on page
Copy editor: Ritchey Halphen
Proofreader: Emily Beaumont
Indexer: Rich Carlson

Library of Congress Cataloging-in-Publication Data

Names: Marlin, Seth, 1983– author.
Title: Five-star trails, Spokane : 30 spectacular hikes in the inland Northwest / Seth Marlin.
Description: First edition. | Birmingham, Alabama : Menasha Ridge Press, 2020. | Includes index.
Identifiers: LCCN 2019057543 (pbk.) | LCCN 2019057544 (ebook) | ISBN 978-1-63404-134-8
(pbk.) | ISBN 978-1-63404-135-5 (ebook)
Subjects: LCSH: Hiking—Washington (State)—Spokane Region—Guidebooks | Trails—Washington
(State)—Spokane Region—Guidebooks | Spokane Region (Wash.)—Guidebooks.
Classification: LCC GV199.42.W22 S646 2020 (pbk.) | LCC GV199.42.W22 (ebook) | DDC
796.5109797/772—dc23
LC record available at lccn.loc.gov/2019057543
LC ebook record available at lccn.loc.gov/2019057544

 MENASHA RIDGE PRESS
An imprint of AdventureKEEN
2204 First Ave. S., Ste. 102
Birmingham, AL 35233
800-443-7227, fax 205-326-1012

Visit menasharidge.com for a complete listing of our books and for ordering information. Contact us at our
website, at facebook.com/menasharidge, or at twitter.com/menasharidge with questions or comments. To find
out more about who we are and what we're doing, visit blog.menasharidge.com.

Frontispiece: Indian Painted Rocks Trail *(see Hike 8, page 59)*
Cover photos: (front) Mineral Ridge National Recreation Trail *(see Hike 27, page 168)*; (back) Beacon Hill
Bike Park Loop *(see Hike 20, page 124)*

SAFETY NOTICE Though the author and publisher have made every effort to ensure that the information in
this book is accurate at press time, they are not responsible for any loss, damage, injury, or inconvenience that
may occur while using this book—you are responsible for your own safety and health on the trail. The fact
that a hike is described in this book does not mean that it will be safe for you. Always check local conditions
(which can change from day to day), know your own limitations, and consult a map.

For the latest information about places in this book that have been affected by the coronavirus,
please consult the "Contacts" and "Nearby Attractions" listings in the hike profiles, as well as Appendixes A
and C (pages 190 and 192). For general news and updates about the coronavirus in Washington State and
Idaho, check coronavirus.wa.gov and coronavirus.idaho.gov.

Table of Contents

City Center 91

Spokane Valley 119

Mount Spokane State Park 147

Northern Idaho 167

Dedication

For my son, David, and my daughter, Catherine. I love you with all my heart.

Acknowledgments

THANKS FIRST OF ALL TO MENASHA RIDGE PRESS for the opportunity to work together on producing this guide; special credit goes to Brett Ortler and Tim Jackson for all their hard work and editorial support. Additional thanks goes to Holly Weiler for her insights into Washington state park trails and to Ellie Kozlowski for her guidance on the writing and submissions process. All creative ventures are ultimately collaborative, and I've been lucky enough to rely on some truly amazing people.

Additional mention goes to Washington State Parks for its tireless work in keeping the Evergreen State beautiful. Likewise, Spokane County Parks, Recreation & Golf has done great work in making the Lilac City a prime place to hike and explore. Thanks as well to the Idaho Department of Natural Resources—their hard work is reflected in the stunning beauty of the trails throughout the Idaho panhandle. I feel that we don't show enough appreciation for the rangers and volunteers who maintain our public lands, and I can't express my thanks enough.

I would be remiss, of course, in not mentioning the amazing education and mentorship I've received. To that end, I wish to thank the English Department at Boise State University and the MFA Program in Creative Writing at Eastern Washington University. Particular thanks goes to Alan Heathcock and Sam Ligon for their encouragement.

Finally, I have so many people in my personal life to thank for their support. My parents, Richard and Patricia, have always encouraged me in my dreams of being a writer. I also owe a shout-out to Elizabeth for her patience and understanding. And last of all, I'd like to thank Jane Mayes, whose love and friendship helped guide me down this path in the first place.

—*Seth Marlin*

Preface

WELCOME TO THIS FIVE-STAR TRAILS GUIDE to day hikes in and around Spokane! While perhaps not as well known as some areas west of the Cascades, the Inland Northwest possesses a charm and an ecology all its own. I've lived here for close to a decade now, and I enjoy it so much that I chose to start a family here.

My love of hiking was instilled from an early age—when I was growing up in my native Michigan, long walks through the woods with my father were a major part of my upbringing. This proximity to nature proved formative for me, and it has given me an appreciation of the outdoors that remains with me to this day. After moving to Spokane in 2011 to pursue graduate studies at Eastern Washington University, I found a few kindred spirits within the English department there. Over the years that followed, my fellow grad-school buddies and I would meet up every few months to hike nearby trails in the area. Our treks ranged far and wide, from Lakeview Ranch out near Odessa to Bead Lake and Farragut State Park along the Washington–Idaho border. While not every one of these hikes would be ideal for a family outing, I learned quickly about all that this amazing region has to offer.

Contrasted with the temperate forests and snowcapped ranges of the Cascades, Eastern Washington might be easy to dismiss as relatively bleak and flat if you're unfamiliar with the area. But nothing could be further from the truth: the Inland Northwest possesses remarkable variety in both geography and biodiversity, so whether you prefer well-kept trails close to town or mountain solitude far from fellow humans, you're sure to find something to love just a short drive away.

As the second-largest city in Washington State, Spokane rests in the center of a broad valley, at the intersection of several distinct biomes. To the north lie the Selkirk Mountains, cool and heavily forested; to the east, the Rocky Mountain foothills; to the south, the rolling prairies of the Palouse; and to the west, the high scrublands of the Columbia River Basin.

To the casual observer, a survey of local history evokes images of Lewis and Clark, of pioneer gumption and the settlers who tamed an untamable wilderness. In reality, the history of human settlement in the region stretches back thousands of years, to a time when Columbian mammoths and giant ground

LOOKING NORTH ON THE MEDICAL LAKE LOOP (SEE HIKE 3, PAGE 34)

sloths foraged along the banks of the Spokane River. Indigenous tribes, including the Coeur d'Alene, Kalispel, Kootenai, Nez Perce, and Spokane, have lived here since well before European explorers arrived. These tribes' varied histories and traditions have all left their mark upon the region, both in terms of art and culture as well as respect for the land and its wildlife. As much as cities like Seattle or Portland value their history and connections to nature, so too does Spokane.

Although the hikes in this guide vary by region and degree of difficulty, I've selected all of them for their proximity to town, family friendliness, trail conditions, and unique features. Whether you're searching for a day hike with the kids or a strenuous solo trek to clear the head and build up the calf muscles, you'll be sure to find something perfect for your needs within these pages.

It's been my pleasure to put together this book, and it's my honor now to share my findings with you. Happy hiking!

—S. M.

Recommended Hikes

Best for Accessibility

Best for Bird-Watching

Best for Berry-Picking

Best for Urban Convenience

Best for Dogs

Best for Exercise

Best for Fall Color

Best for Geology

Best for Kids

Best for Solitude

Best for Views

Best for Wildlife

Map Legend

←→ ➡ Directional arrows	Featured trail	Alternate trail
Freeway	Highway with bridge	Minor road
Boardwalk	Stairs	Unpaved road
Railroad	Power line	
Park/forest	Water body	River/creek/ intermittent stream/wash

🏃 Baseball field	🏌 Golf course	Radio tower
Basketball court	Information/kiosk	Restrooms
Beach access	⚓ Marina	RV campground
Boat launch	Marsh	Scenic view
Dam	⚒ Mine	Ski lift
Drinking water	P Parking	Swimming access
Electrical tower	▲ Peak	Tennis court
Footbridge	Picnic area	Trailhead
Gate	Picnic shelter	Tunnel (road)
General point of interest	Playground	Waterfall

 # Introduction

About This Book

I'VE ORGANIZED THE TRAILS IN THIS BOOK REGIONALLY, following an east–west line, as follows: **West Plains, West Spokane, City Center, Spokane Valley, Mount Spokane State Park,** and **Northern Idaho.** Below I discuss the individual regions and their hiking highlights.

West Plains

This area about 10 minutes west of Spokane, which consists mostly of prairie scrub and assorted wetlands, is part of a region known as the Channeled Scablands that covers much of Eastern Washington. Best approached in the cool temperatures of spring, when the wildflowers are in bloom, the West Plains boast scenic views and great opportunities for bird-watching. Noteworthy hiking spots in this area include the Medical Lake Loop (see Hike 3, page 34) and the trails in Turnbull National Wildlife Refuge (see Hikes 4–6, pages 38, 42, and 47).

West Spokane

Just across Latah Creek from the city of Spokane, this region stretches from Vinegar Flats all the way north to Nine Mile Falls. The area—which becomes more wooded as you draw closer to town—includes a number of local and state parks, among them Palisades Park, People's Park, and Riverside State Park. The trails here are known for being family-friendly, close to the water, and well marked, with ample opportunities for rock-climbing, swimming, and even disc golf. Popular hikes in this area include the Indian Painted Rocks Trail (see Hikes 7 and 8, pages 54 and 59), the Bowl and Pitcher Loop (see Hike 11, page 73), and the Deep Creek Canyon Loop (see Hike 12, page 78).

City Center

Straddling the banks of the mighty Spokane River, the beating heart of downtown Spokane boasts a surprising number of hiking opportunities, among them the Hangman Park Loop (see Hike 15, page 97) as well as a large stretch of the 38-mile Centennial Trail (see Hike 17, page 107) and the Spokane River Walk (see Hike 18, page 112). These hikes are great for both pets and families, as they tend to be short and offer ready access to fine dining, arts festivals, and open-air markets. They're great for an afternoon stroll while you're visiting town.

Spokane Valley

Situated east of Spokane proper and stretching all the way to the border with Idaho, this area features a number of amazing hikes, among them the loops in Antoine Peak Conservation Area (see Hike 19, page 120) and Liberty Lake Regional Park (see Hike 23, page 139), as well as all of the hikes within the scenic Dishman Hills Conservation Area (see Hikes 21 and 22, pages 129 and 134). Depending on whether you're north or south of I-90, you can find stunning views of nearby Mount Spokane (see the next region) and Micah Peak, along with the Rocks of Sharon and the rolling grasslands known as the Palouse. The parks in this area are largely county-maintained and offer treks of moderate difficulty.

Mount Spokane State Park

Located north of Spokane Valley, this state park is named for the dome-shaped peak that dominates the surrounding landscape. The park, which can be accessed only on a series of winding roads, offers opportunities for quaint country dining along with visits to a few local orchards and meaderies. Mount Spokane is crisscrossed by a massive network of trails, among them Trail 100 (see Hike 25, page 155) and the infamous Summit Loop (see Hike 24, page 148). Visitors can expect stunning views of the entire Spokane Valley, as well as opportunities for wildlife-watching and berry-picking. Be warned, though: the trails here are accessible only in season, suffer from poor cell reception, and are among the most physically strenuous of any in this guide. These hikes are best for seasoned travelers and families with older children, and they're best experienced from spring through early fall.

Northern Idaho

Encompassing the easternmost part of metro Spokane, this region includes the cities of Coeur d'Alene and Post Falls and features some of the best wilderness hiking in this guide. Northern Idaho boasts cooler weather and greater plant diversity than you might find to the west, plus vast expanses of pine forest. Be sure to check out the Mineral Ridge National Recreation Trail (see Hike 27, page 168) or, if you're looking for an in-town jaunt, the interpretive trail at Tubbs Hill (see Hike 30, page 185).

How to Use This Guidebook

The following section walks you through this book's organization, making it easy and convenient to plan great hikes.

The Overview Map, Overview Map Key, and Legend

The overview map (page ii) shows the trailheads for all 30 hikes; the numbers on this map pair with the key on the facing page. A legend explaining the symbols used on the trail maps (see below) is found on page xii.

Trail Maps

In addition to the overview map on the inside cover, a detailed map of each hike's route appears with its profile. On each of these maps, symbols indicate the trailhead, the complete route, significant features, facilities, and topographic landmarks such as creeks, overlooks, and peaks.

FOOTBRIDGE ON LIBERTY LAKE LOOP, LOOKING SOUTH (SEE HIKE 23, PAGE 139)

To produce the highly accurate maps in this book, I used a handheld GPS unit to gather data while hiking each route, then sent that data to Menasha Ridge Press's expert cartographers. Be aware, though, that your GPS device is no substitute for sound, sensible navigation that takes into account the conditions that you observe while hiking.

Elevation Profile

Except for a handful of fairly flat routes, each hike includes this diagram in addition to a trail map. Each entry's key information also lists the elevation at the hike's low and high points.

The elevation profile represents the rises and falls of the trail as viewed from the side, over the complete distance (in miles) of that trail. On the diagram's vertical axis, or height scale, the number of feet indicated between each tick mark lets you visualize the climb. To avoid making flat hikes look steep and steep hikes appear flat, varying height scales provide an accurate image of each hike's climbing challenge.

The Hike Profile

Each profile opens with the hike's star ratings, GPS trailhead coordinates, and other at-a-glance information. Each profile also includes a map (see "Trail Maps" on the previous page). The main text for each profile includes four sections: Overview, Route Details, Nearby Attractions (where applicable), and Directions (for driving to the trailhead area).

STAR RATINGS

The hikes in *Five-Star Trails: Spokane* were carefully chosen to provide an overall five-star experience, and they represent the diversity of trails found in the region. Each hike was assigned a one- to five-star rating in each of the following categories: scenery, trail condition, suitability for children, level of difficulty, and degree of solitude. While one hike may merit five stars for its stunning scenery, that same trail may rank as a two-star trail for children. Similarly, another hike might receive two stars for difficulty but earn five stars for solitude. It's rare that any trail receives five stars in all five categories; nevertheless, each trail offers excellence in at least one category, if not others.

Here's how the star ratings for each of the five categories break down:

FOR SCENERY:

★ ★ ★ ★ ★	Unique, picturesque panoramas
★ ★ ★ ★	Diverse vistas
★ ★ ★	Pleasant views
★ ★	Unchanging landscape
★	Not selected for scenery

FOR TRAIL CONDITION:

★ ★ ★ ★ ★	Consistently well maintained
★ ★ ★ ★	Stable, with no surprises
★ ★ ★	Average terrain to negotiate
★ ★	Inconsistent, with good and poor areas
★	Rocky, overgrown, or often muddy

FOR CHILDREN:

★ ★ ★ ★ ★	Babes in strollers are welcome
★ ★ ★ ★	Fun for any kid past the toddler stage
★ ★ ★	Good for young hikers with proven stamina
★ ★	Not enjoyable for children
★	Not advisable for children

FOR DIFFICULTY:

★ ★ ★ ★ ★	Grueling
★ ★ ★ ★	Strenuous
★ ★ ★	Moderate: won't beat you up—but you'll know you've been hiking
★ ★	Easy, with patches of moderate
★	Good for a relaxing stroll

FOR SOLITUDE:

★ ★ ★ ★ ★	Positively tranquil
★ ★ ★ ★	Spurts of isolation
★ ★ ★	Moderately secluded
★ ★	Crowded on weekends and holidays
★	Steady stream of individuals and/or groups

GPS TRAILHEAD COORDINATES

As noted in "Trail Maps" (page 3), I used a handheld GPS unit to obtain geographic data and sent the information to the publisher's cartographers. In the opener for each hike profile, the coordinates—the intersection of the latitude (north) and longitude (west)—will orient you from the trailhead. In some cases, you can drive within viewing distance of a trailhead. Other hiking routes require a short walk to the trailhead from a parking area.

This guidebook expresses GPS coordinates in degree–decimal minute format. For example, the coordinates for Hike 1, Columbia Plateau State Park Trail: Cheney Trailhead to Fish Lake (page 24), are as follows:

N47° 28.762' W117° 33.642'

The latitude–longitude grid system is likely quite familiar to you, but here's a refresher, pertinent to visualizing the coordinates:

Imaginary lines of latitude—called parallels and approximately 69 miles apart from each other—run horizontally around the globe. The equator is established to be 0°, and each parallel is indicated by degrees from the equator: up to 90°N at the North Pole and down to 90°S at the South Pole.

Imaginary lines of longitude—called meridians—run perpendicular to latitude lines. Longitude lines are likewise indicated by degrees. Starting from 0° at the Prime Meridian in Greenwich, England, they continue to the east and west until they meet 180° later at the International Date Line in the Pacific Ocean. At the equator, longitude lines also are approximately 69 miles apart, but that distance narrows as the meridians converge toward the North and South Poles.

To convert GPS coordinates given in degrees, minutes, and seconds to degree–decimal minute format, divide the seconds by 60. For more information about GPS technology, see usgs.gov.

DISTANCE AND CONFIGURATION

Distance notes the length of the hike round-trip, from start to finish. If the hike description includes options to shorten or extend the hike, those round-trip distances are also included here. **Configuration** defines the type of route—for example, an out-and-back (which takes you in and out the same way), a point-to-point (or one-way route), a figure-eight, or a balloon.

HIKING TIME

Two miles per hour is a general rule of thumb for the hiking times noted in this guidebook. That pace typically allows time for taking photos, for dawdling and admiring views, and for alternating stretches of hills and descents. When deciding whether or not to follow a particular trail in this guidebook, consider the weather, plus your own pace, general physical condition, and energy level on a given day.

HIGHLIGHTS

Describes features that draw hikers to the trail: mountain or forest views, water features, historical sites, and the like.

ELEVATION

Each hike's key information lists the elevation at the trail's low and high points. Most hikes also include an elevation profile (see page 4).

ACCESS

Trail-access hours are listed here, along with any applicable fees or permits required to hike the trail.

MAPS

Recommendations for maps, in addition to those in this guidebook, are listed here. As noted earlier, we advise that you carry more than one map—and that you consult those maps before heading out on the trail in order to resolve any confusion or discrepancy.

FACILITIES

Includes visitor centers, restrooms, water, picnic tables, and other basics at or near the trailhead.

WHEELCHAIR ACCESS

Notes paved sections or other areas where one can safely use a wheelchair.

COMMENTS

Here you'll find assorted nuggets of information, such as advice on attempting a given hike under off-season weather conditions.

CONTACTS

Listed here are phone numbers, websites, and email addresses for checking trail conditions and gleaning other day-to-day information.

Overview, Route Details, Nearby Attractions, and Directions

These four elements compose the heart of the hike. **Overview** gives you a quick summary of what to expect on that trail; **Route Details** guides you on the hike, from start to finish; and **Nearby Attractions** suggests appealing adjacent sites, such as restaurants, museums, and other trails (note that not every hike has this listing). **Directions** will get you to the trailhead from a well-known road or highway.

BEN BURR TRAIL (SEE HIKE 14, PAGE 92)

Weather

Hiking in Spokane is a popular hobby, with a variety of trails accessible year-round. Every season here has something to offer.

For those who are plotting desert hikes or are otherwise planning to beat the heat, springtime offers some lovely opportunities for outdoor recreation. Wildflowers bloom all across the West Plains, and the days themselves range from balmy and sun-drenched to cool and rainy.

Of course, what would summer be without the odd weekend excursion? The period from June to early September brings in visitors from across the state and beyond, eager to soak up some sun and cool off in one of the region's numerous lakes or rivers. Summers in the Spokane area are generally hot and dry, so be sure to bring extra water and, as always, pay attention to any burn bans posted in the area—fire safety is everyone's responsibility.

Fall is my favorite time to hike in Spokane. The days retain their sunny character from the preceding season, but they also bring with them a briskness that suits a vigorous trek through the woods. The aspen, locust, ash, and maple trees of the region put on a blazing display of color, and even the Western larch gets in on the act, being one of the few coniferous trees to seasonally shed its needles. Fall visitors to spots such as Mount Spokane will find the treetops draped in fiery gold, making for some fantastic photo opportunities.

It would be easy to dismiss winter as a poor time to hike, but in reality Spokane's relatively low snowfall makes for some promising treks for hardy souls. While it's wisest to save the higher-altitude trails for summertime, the lower-elevation hikes, particularly those in the West Plains and West Spokane, are generally dry and well packed. Be sure to dress in layers, and carry extra first aid supplies such as reflective thermal blankets and fire-starting gear. Hypothermia is no joke: it can claim even the savviest of hikers.

The table below lists average temperatures and precipitation by month for the greater Spokane region. For each month, "Hi Temp" is the average daytime high, "Lo Temp" is the average nighttime low, and "Rain or Snow" is the average amount of precipitation (in inches).

MONTH	HI TEMP	LO TEMP	RAIN OR SNOW
January	34°F	25°F	1.77" (11" of snow)
February	40°F	26°F	1.34" (7" of snow)
March	49°F	32°F	1.61" (4" of snow)
April	57°F	37°F	1.30"
May	66°F	44°F	1.61"
June	74°F	50°F	1.26"
July	83°F	56°F	0.63"
August	83°F	56°F	0.63"
September	73°F	47°F	0.67"
October	58°F	37°F	1.18"
November	42°F	30°F	2.28" (7" of snow)
December	32°F	22°F	2.28" (15" of snow)

Source: usclimatedata.com

Water

A hiker walking steadily in 90° heat needs about 10 quarts of fluid per day. That's 2.5 gallons—12 large water bottles or 16 small ones. A good rule of thumb is to hydrate before your hike, carry (and drink) 6 ounces of water for every mile you plan to hike, and hydrate again after the hike.

For most people, the pleasures of hiking make the burden of carrying water a relatively minor inconvenience, so pack more water than you think you'll need, even for short hikes. If you don't like drinking tepid water on a hot day, freeze a couple of bottles overnight. It's also a good idea to carry a bottle of sports drink such as Gatorade; the electrolytes replace essential salts that you sweat out.

If you find yourself tempted to drink so-called found water, proceed with extreme caution. Many ponds and lakes you'll encounter are fairly stagnant, and the water tastes terrible. Drinking such water presents inherent risks for thirsty trekkers. *Giardia* parasites contaminate many water sources and can cause giardiasis, an extremely painful gastric ailment that can last for weeks after onset. For more information, visit the Centers for Disease Control and Prevention website: cdc.gov/parasites/giardia.

In any case, effective treatment is essential before you use any water source found along the trail. Boiling water for 2–3 minutes is always a safe measure for camping, but day hikers can consider iodine tablets, approved chemical mixes, filtration units rated for giardia, and ultraviolet filtration. Some of these methods (for example, filtration with an added carbon filter) remove bad tastes typical in stagnant water, while others add their own taste. As a precaution, carry a means of water purification in case you've underestimated your consumption needs.

Clothing

Weather, unexpected trail conditions, fatigue, extended hiking duration, and wrong turns can individually or collectively turn a great outing into a very uncomfortable one at best—and a life-threatening one at worst. Thus, proper attire plays a key role in staying comfortable and, sometimes, staying alive. Here are some helpful guidelines:

* Choose silk, wool, or synthetics for maximum comfort in all of your hiking attire— from hats to socks and in between. Cotton is fine if the weather remains dry and stable, not so much if that material gets wet.

* Always wear a hat, or at least tuck one into your day pack or hitch it to your belt. Hats offer all-weather sun and wind protection as well as warmth if it turns cold.

* Be ready to layer up or down as the day progresses and the mercury rises or falls. Today's outdoor wear makes layering easy, with such designs as jackets that convert to vests and zip-off or button-up legs.

* Wear hiking boots or sturdy hiking sandals with toe protection. Flip-flopping on a paved path in an urban botanical garden is one thing, but never hike mountain trails

in open sandals or casual sneakers. Your bones and arches need support, and your skin needs protection.

★ Pair that footwear with good socks. If you prefer not to sheathe your feet when wearing hiking sandals, tuck the socks into your day pack; you may need them if the weather plummets or if you hit rocky turf and pebbles begin to irritate your feet. And if you've lost your gloves, you can wear the socks as mittens in a pinch.

★ Don't leave rainwear behind, even if the day dawns clear and sunny. Tuck into your day pack, or tie around your waist, a jacket that is breathable and either water-resistant or waterproof. Investigate different choices at your local outdoors retailer. If you're a frequent hiker, ideally you'll have more than one rainwear weight, material, and style in your closet to protect you in all seasons in your regional climate and hiking microclimates.

Essential Gear

Today you can buy outdoor vests that have up to 20 pockets shaped and sized to carry everything from toothpicks to binoculars. Or, if you don't aspire to feel like a burro, you can neatly stow all of the following items in your day pack or backpack:

★ *Extra clothes:* raingear, a change of socks and shirt, and depending on the season, a warm hat and gloves.

★ *Extra food:* trail mix, granola bars, or other high-energy snacks.

★ *Flashlight or headlamp* with extra bulb and batteries, for getting back to the trailhead if you take longer than expected.

★ *Insect repellent* to ward off ticks and other biting bugs.

★ *Maps and a high-quality compass.* Even if you know the terrain from previous hikes, don't leave home without these tools. And, as previously noted, bring maps in addition to those in this guidebook, and consult your maps prior to the hike. If you own a GPS unit, bring that too, but don't rely on it as your sole navigational tool—batteries can die, after all.

The latest smartphones not only enable you to call for help but also have built-in GPS hardware and software that can help with orientation. (Don't call for help, though, unless you truly need it—remember that your phone's battery can die too.) Smartphones are also valuable for downloading maps to use on the trail, although it's always better to download a map *before* your hike rather than trying to do so on the fly, as coverage can be unreliable in the mountains near Spokane.

★ *Pocketknife and/or multitool.*

★ *Sun protection:* sunglasses with UV tinting, a sunhat with a wide brim, and sunscreen. (*Tip:* Check the expiration date on the tube or bottle.)

★ *Water.* Again, bring more than you think you'll drink. Depending on your destination, you may want to bring a container and iodine or a filter for purifying water in case you run out.

★ *Whistle.* It could become your best friend in an emergency.

★ *Windproof matches and/or a lighter,* for real emergencies—please don't start a forest fire.

First Aid Kit

In addition to the preceding items, those that follow may seem daunting to carry along for a day hike. But any paramedic will tell you that the products listed here—again, in alphabetical order, because all are important—are just the basics. The reality of hiking is that you can be out for a week of backpacking and acquire only a mosquito bite. Or you can hike for an hour, slip, and suffer a cut or broken bone. Fortunately, the items listed pack into a very small space. You may also purchase convenient prepackaged kits at your pharmacy or online.

★ Adhesive bandages (such as Band-Aids)

★ Antibiotic ointment (such as Neosporin)

★ Aspirin, acetaminophen (Tylenol), or ibuprofen (Advil)

★ Athletic tape

★ Blister kit (moleskin or an adhesive variety such as Spenco 2nd Skin)

★ Butterfly-closure bandages

★ Diphenhydramine (Benadryl), in case of allergic reactions

★ Elastic bandages (such as Ace) or joint wraps (such as Spenco)

★ Epinephrine in a prefilled syringe (EpiPen), typically by prescription only, for people known to have severe allergic reactions

★ Gauze (one roll and a half-dozen 4-by-4-inch pads)

★ Hydrogen peroxide or iodine

Note: Consider your intended terrain and the number of hikers in your party before you exclude any article listed above. A short stroll may not inspire you to carry a complete kit, but anything beyond that warrants precaution. When hiking alone, you should always be prepared for a medical need. And if you're a twosome or a group, one or more people in your party should be equipped with first aid supplies.

General Safety

Here are a few tips to make your hike safer and easier:

★ *Always let someone know where you'll be hiking and how long you expect to be gone.* It's a good idea to give that person a copy of your route, particularly if you're headed into an isolated area. Let him or her know when you return.

★ *Always sign in and out of any trail registers provided.* Don't hesitate to comment on the trail condition if space is provided; that's your opportunity to alert others to any problems you encounter.

★ *Don't count on a mobile phone for your safety.* Reception may be spotty or nonexistent on the trail.

★ *Always carry food and water, even for a short hike.* And bring more water than you think you'll need.

★ *Ask questions.* Public-land employees are on hand to help. It's a lot easier to solicit advice before a problem occurs, and it will help you avoid a mishap away from civilization when it's too late to amend an error.

★ *Stay on designated trails.* Even on the most clearly marked trails, you usually reach a point where you have to stop and consider in which direction to head. If you become disoriented, don't panic. As soon as you think you may be off-track, stop, assess your current direction, and then retrace your steps to the point where you went astray. Using a map (paper or digital), a compass, a GPS or smartphone, and this book, and keeping in mind what you've passed thus far, reorient yourself, and trust your judgment on which way to continue. If you become absolutely unsure of how to continue, return to your vehicle the way you came in. Should you become completely lost and have no idea how to find the trailhead, remaining in place along the trail and waiting for help is most often the best option for adults and always the best option for children.

★ *Always carry a whistle.* It may become a lifesaver if you get lost or hurt.

★ *Be especially careful when crossing streams.* Whether you're fording the stream or crossing on a log, make every step count. If you have any doubt about maintaining your balance on a log, ford the stream instead: use a trekking pole or stout stick for balance, and *face upstream as you cross*. If a stream seems too deep to ford, turn back. Whatever is on the other side isn't worth the risk.

★ *Be careful at overlooks.* While these areas may provide spectacular views, they are potentially hazardous. Stay back from the edge of outcrops, and make absolutely sure of your footing—a misstep can mean a nasty and possibly fatal fall.

★ *Standing dead trees and storm-damaged living trees pose a significant hazard to hikers.* These trees may have loose or broken limbs that could fall at any time. While walking beneath trees, and when choosing a spot to rest or enjoy your snack, *look up*.

★ *Know the symptoms of subnormal body temperature, or hypothermia.* Shivering and forgetfulness are the two most common indicators of this stealthy killer. Hypothermia can occur at any elevation, even in the summer, especially if you're wearing lightweight cotton clothing. If symptoms develop, get to shelter, hot liquids, and dry clothes as soon as possible.

★ *Likewise, know the symptoms of heat exhaustion, or hyperthermia.* Here's how to recognize and handle three types of heat emergencies:

Heat cramps are painful cramps in the legs and abdomen, accompanied by heavy sweating and feeling faint. Caused by excessive salt loss, heat cramps must be handled by getting to a cool place and sipping water or an electrolyte solution (such as Gatorade).

Dizziness, headache, irregular pulse, disorientation, and nausea are all symptoms of **heat exhaustion,** which occurs as blood vessels dilate and attempt to move heat from the inner body to the skin. Find a cool place, drink cool water, and get a friend to fan you, which can help cool you off more quickly.

Heatstroke is a life-threatening condition that can cause convulsions, unconsciousness, or even death. Symptoms include dilated pupils; dry, hot, flushed skin; a rapid pulse; high fever; and abnormal breathing. If you should be sweating and you're not, that's the signature warning sign. If you or a hiking partner is experiencing heatstroke, do whatever you can to cool down and find help.

★ *Most importantly, take along your brain.* A cool, calculating mind is the single most important asset on the trail. Think before you act. Watch your step. Plan ahead. Avoiding accidents before they happen is the best way to ensure a rewarding and relaxing hike.

Watchwords for Flora and Fauna

Hikers should be aware of the following concerns regarding plants and wildlife, described in alphabetical order.

BLACK BEARS Though attacks are uncommon, the sight or approach of a bear can give anyone a start. In Washington, black bears can be found in wooded areas, particularly wherever wild berries such as currants and huckleberries grow.

If you encounter a bear up close while hiking, remain calm and resist the urge to run. Make loud noises to scare off the bear, and back away slowly. In primitive and remote areas, assume that bears are present; in more-developed sites, check on the current bear situation before you hike. Most encounters are food-related, as bears have an exceptional sense of smell and not particularly discriminating tastes. While this is of greater concern to backpackers and campers, on a day hike, you may want to enjoy a lunchtime picnic or munch on an energy bar or other snack from time to time, so remain aware and alert.

BLACKFLIES Also known locally as deer flies, these pests present a particularly vicious nuisance, although thankfully the worst they'll cause is an itchy welt. Blackflies are most active mid-May–June during the day and especially before thunderstorms, as well as during the morning and evening. Insect repellent can help, but the only way to keep out of the flies' swarming midst is to keep moving.

DEER are a common sight in Eastern Washington, both the familiar white-tailed kind as well as the smaller mule deer (so named for its prominent ears). They favor large, open fields as well as deep stands of pine and cedar, particularly in winter when food becomes scarce. Human encroachment in recent years, however, has forced deer into urban areas, where they've been spotted grazing on people's lawns and even their prize flower bushes.

WHITE-TAILED DEER
photographed by RT Images/Shutterstock

Though deer are generally timid, bucks (males) may occasionally become aggressive when competing for mates. In most cases, clapping your hands and shouting will drive them off, although if you encounter a buck that stands its ground—perhaps by stomping its front hooves for emphasis—it would be wise to move away. Additionally, does are known to leave their fawns in tall brush while they go off to forage, so if you come upon a baby that seems to be unattended, don't fret; leave it alone and continue on your way.

ELK are a rare sight for most hikers, although on the slopes of Mount Spokane and east into Northern Idaho, they can occasionally be found moving in large herds. Typically they keep to mountainsides and tree stands to graze, moving downhill in the predawn hours in search of water. They generally aren't territorial and prefer to avoid human contact, though it would be wise to steer clear during the September–October mating season.

MOOSE Larger even than the formidable elk—growing as tall as 12 feet at the shoulder—moose are generally solitary creatures, though their imposing size makes them difficult to miss. Generally reclusive, they can be found wandering alone or with young, in deeply wooded areas close to riverbanks. Unlike elk, moose are extremely territorial, and bulls signal threats either by thrashing their antlers from side to side or by charging aggressively. In any case, these creatures are not to be trifled with: back away slowly in case of an encounter, and be sure to notify the Washington Department of Fish & Wildlife (360-902-2200).

MOSQUITOES Keep these pests at bay with insect repellent and/or repellent-infused clothing. Mosquitoes in the Spokane area have been known to carry West Nile virus, so take all due caution to avoid their bites.

MOUNTAIN LIONS Growing up to 150 pounds, these solitary predators aren't generally known to attack humans, but they have occasionally been known to do so if hungry or sick, particularly in the late fall and early spring. They prefer wooded upland areas, hiding out in small caves or burrows, and like all big cats, they're masters of using their environment to mask their presence. This talent, coupled with their tendency to avoid humans unless under duress, means that on the rare occasions that you encounter them, it's usually a sign of trouble.

Dogs can be helpful in alerting you to the presence of mountain lions nearby; as always, however, you should leash your dog to keep it safe. It's also a good idea to carry pepper spray or bear spray, which you can buy at any sporting goods store and readily clip to your pack.

In most cases these cats will usually turn tail and flee, but if they stand their ground and maintain eye contact, then you'll need to take action. Some guidelines:

* *Keep children close to you, or hold your child.* Observed in captivity, mountain lions seem especially drawn to small children.

* *Do not approach a mountain lion.* Instead, give it room to get away.

* *Try to make yourself look larger* by raising your arms and opening your jacket if you're wearing one.

* *Don't crouch or kneel.* It could make you seem smaller and more vulnerable.

* *Act like the predator, not the prey.* With as little movement as possible, gather nearby stones or branches and toss them at the animal. Slowly wave your arms above your head, and speak in a firm voice.

★ *If all else fails and you get attacked, fight back.* Hikers have successfully fought off mountain lions with rocks and sticks. Try to remain facing the animal, and fend off attempts to bite at your head or neck.

Once the threat has passed, notify the Washington Department of Fish & Wildlife (360-902-2200).

POISON IVY photographed by Tom Watson

POISON IVY Recognizing and avoiding poison ivy (*right*) are the most effective ways to prevent painful, itchy rashes. The plant occurs as a vine or ground cover, three leaflets per leaf (for reference, remember the classic maxim "Leaves of three, let them be"). Urushiol, the oil in the plant, is responsible for the rash. Within 14 hours of exposure, raised lines and/or blisters will appear on the affected area, accompanied by a terrible itch. Try to refrain from scratching, because bacteria under your fingernails can cause an infection. Wash and dry the affected area thoroughly with soap and water or a product such as Tecnu; then apply calamine lotion and/or an anti-itch cream. If itching or blistering is severe, seek medical attention. Likewise, make sure to wash any clothes, pets, or hiking gear that may have come in contact with the plant—you could experience a second breakout months after the first if you put on a shirt or a pair of boots that were never properly cleaned.

WESTERN RATTLESNAKE
photographed by Robert Mutch/Shutterstock

SNAKES Roughly a dozen different snake species inhabit Washington State. The only venomous kind, however, is the western rattlesnake (*right*), which is common in the high scrublands of the West Plains and in upland regions as far east as Northern Idaho, wherever available burrows and decent sun exposure can be found.

Sometimes described as the gentlemen of snakes, rattlers tend to keep to themselves, leaving their burrows only to sun themselves and hunt. They are most generally encountered in early mornings during the summer months, are slow to provoke, and will generally alert you by rattling before they strike, though this temperamental quirk shouldn't be taken as an invitation to cuddle up. The best rule is to leave all snakes alone, regardless of species.

When hiking, stick to well-used trails, and wear over-the-ankle boots and loose-fitting long pants. Don't step or put your hands where you can't see, and avoid wandering around in the dark. Step *onto* logs and rocks, never *over* them, and be especially careful when climbing rocks. Avoid walking through dense brush. Finally, don't peer into animal burrows, and make sure that dogs don't either.

DEER TICK   photographed by Jim Gathany/Centers for Disease Control and Prevention (public domain)

TICKS These arachnids are often found in brush and tall grass, where they wait to hitch a ride on warm-blooded passersby. Adult ticks are most active April–May and again in October–November. The black-legged tick (*left*), commonly called the deer tick, is the primary carrier of Lyme disease.

When you're on the trail, wear light-colored clothing to make it easier to spot ticks before they can burrow in. Afterward, visually check hair, the back of the neck, armpits, and socks. Run your clothes through a dryer cycle to kill any stragglers, and take a moment during your posthike shower to do a more complete check of your entire body. Use tweezers to remove ticks that are already attached: grasp the tick close to the skin, and pull it straight out rather than twisting. Thoroughly clean the bite and your hands with disinfectant solution or soap and water. If you later feel ill or a red, ringlike rash develops where the tick was embedded, see a doctor.

Hunting

Different rules and licenses govern the various hunting types and related seasons. You may wish to forgo trips during times when the woods fill with blaze orange and camouflage as well as the sounds of gunfire. The hunting seasons for Washington State are as follows:

BEARS August–November (varies by region)

DEER September–October

ELK August–January (varies by region)

MIGRATORY WATERFOWL September–October (varies by region)

MOUNTAIN LIONS September–December

SMALL GAME September–March (varies by animal)

UPLAND GAME BIRDS September–January (varies by animal)

WILD TURKEYS April–May

For additional information, please visit the Washington Department of Fish & Wildlife website: wdfw.wa.gov/hunting/regulations.

Other Regulations

Public-land rules vary by region and municipality, but a few general guidelines apply consistently across the board:

★ *Dispose of trash in provided receptacles, or pack it in and pack it out.* Help keep Eastern Washington's natural areas clean and beautiful.

★ *Dogs should be leashed on every hike in this book where they're allowed.* As a general rule, leashes should be no more than 8 feet long. Also, please pick up after your dog, bag all waste, and dispose of it in on-site trash cans.

★ *Burn bans are extremely common during the Eastern Washington wildfire season,* which typically runs May–October. Don't build campfires, smoke, or set off fireworks where signage prohibits it.

Trail Etiquette

Always treat trails, wildlife, and your fellow hikers with respect. Here are a few reminders.

★ *Plan ahead in order to be self-sufficient at all times.* For example, carry necessary supplies for changes in weather or other conditions. A well-planned trip brings satisfaction to you and to others.

★ *Hike on open trails only.*

★ *Check conditions before you head out* if you think road or trail closures may be a possibility (use the websites or phone numbers listed in the "Contacts" section at the beginning of each hike profile). And don't try to circumvent such closures.

* *Don't trespass on private land,* and obtain all necessary permits and authorization as required. Leave gates as you found them or as directed by signage.

* *Be courteous to other hikers,* bikers, equestrians, and others you encounter on the trails.

* *Never spook wild animals or pets.* An unannounced approach, a sudden movement, or a loud noise startles most critters, and a surprised animal can be dangerous to you, to others, and to itself. Give animals plenty of space.

* *Observe any YIELD signs* you encounter. Typically they advise hikers to yield to horses, and bikers to yield to both horses and hikers. Observing common courtesy on hills, hikers and bikers yield to any uphill traffic. When encountering mounted riders or horsepackers, hikers can courteously step off the trail, on the downhill side if possible. Calmly greet riders before they reach you, and don't dart behind trees. (You'll seem less spooky to the horse if it can see and hear you.) Also, don't pet a horse unless you're invited to do so.

* *Practice **Leave No Trace** principles.* Leave the trail in the same shape you found it in, if not better. See lnt.org for more information.

Tips on Enjoying Hiking in Spokane

When hiking in and around Spokane, the most important thing is to come prepared. Bring adequate supplies of food, water, and first aid equipment for any trip, along with extra pieces of appropriate clothing. Also be sure to take local geography into account—Spokane sits at the junction of several distinct biomes, each with its own unique weather conditions and ecosystems.

For desert hikes, such as those on the West Plains, try to time your trip for early spring, ideally in the morning. Snakes will be less likely to come out to sun while things are still cool, and during the early part of the year many kinds of wildflowers will be in full bloom.

Outside of the Plains, you have a bit more flexibility in how you prepare for a hike. Many parks in the Spokane area are open sunrise–sunset, and most trails are readily accessible March–November. Many trails can even be hiked in winter, although proper layering and footwear are essential. In summer be mindful of fire-risk alerts—the area's ponderosa forests are prone to igniting in the dry heat.

Speaking of fires, recent years have seen a dramatic spike in the frequency and severity of wildfires across Eastern Washington. Causes vary from climate change to the spread of invasive plant species such as cheatgrass, but the result for hikers is the same: weeks of moderate-to-poor air quality, which can make it difficult or even dangerous to attempt any outdoor activity. Be sure to check the air quality before going out, and pack bandannas or even surgical masks in case the winds change. On days when the air quality is poor, children as well as older hikers should remain indoors.

When it comes to high-altitude locations such as Mount Spokane State Park and Dishman Hills Conservation Area, try to time your hikes for mid- to late summer, particularly if the trail you want to tackle is located on the north-facing side of a mountain. Snow can linger on the ground as late as June, rendering the upper elevations of many trails inaccessible. Even in areas where the snow has melted, trail conditions can continue to be muddy for some weeks afterward.

Finally, be aware that the weather in the greater Spokane area becomes significantly cooler and rainier as you move from west to east—a hot day in Cheney or Spokane will be roughly 10° cooler in Coeur d'Alene. Take careful note of this when preparing for any hike, and pack accordingly.

LOOKING NORTH THROUGH THE TREES TOWARD THE SPOKANE RIVER IN IDAHO'S POST FALLS COMMUNITY FOREST (SEE HIKES 28 AND 29, PAGES 173 AND 180)

West Plains

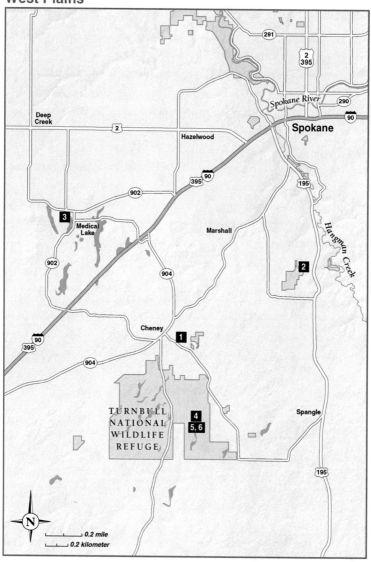

West Plains

THE SOUTHEASTERN LEG OF THE PINE LAKE-HEADQUARTERS LOOP, NEAR STUDY SITE 1
(SEE HIKE 6, PAGE 47)

Columbia Plateau State Park
Trail: Cheney Trailhead to Fish Lake

SCENERY: ★ ★ ★ ★ ★
TRAIL CONDITION: ★ ★ ★ ★ ★
CHILDREN: ★
DIFFICULTY: ★
SOLITUDE: ★ ★ ★

A VIEW OF FISH LAKE, LOOKING NORTHWEST

GPS TRAILHEAD COORDINATES: N47° 28.762' W117° 33.642'

DISTANCE & CONFIGURATION: 7.6-mile out-and-back

HIKING TIME: 2.5 hours

HIGHLIGHTS: Great trail conditions, easy bike access, fantastic bird-watching, and views of Fish Lake

ELEVATION: 2,208' at lowest point, 2,297' at highest

ACCESS: Daily, 6:30 a.m.–sunset; best accessed March–October. A Washington State Parks Discover Pass ($10/day, $30/year) is required for parking.

MAPS: USGS *Cheney;* trail maps at website below and at trailhead

FACILITIES: Restrooms, picnic tables, map board, and paved parking at trailhead

WHEELCHAIR ACCESS: Yes

COMMENTS: 15-mph bicycle speed limit; dogs must be leashed

CONTACTS: Columbia Plateau State Park, 509-465-5064, parks.state.wa.us/490/columbia-plateau-trail

Overview

Named for the high scabland formation that comprises much of Eastern Washington, the 130-mile Columbia Plateau State Park Trail stretches northwest from Pasco all the way up to the college town of Cheney, 20 miles west of Spokane. While conditions and accessibility vary, this hike covers a 3.78-mile section that is paved and bike-friendly, with numerous rest areas and scenic overlooks. It's great for nature lovers of all ages.

Route Details

Begin this hike from the paved parking area for the Cheney Trailhead. Note the abundance of educational displays present near the restrooms. The trailhead for this hike can be deceptive, as the parking area is just east and slightly above the trail itself. To avoid any confusion, backtrack from the parking lot to where it meets the road, then make an immediate right to head down the embankment. The trail should immediately become apparent.

Head north and slightly east up the trail; there are no turnouts or unmarked areas along this route, so getting lost is all but impossible. The trail is marked by high basalt walls on all sides, a testament to the might needed to carve a railroad through this unforgiving landscape. In about 0.3 mile, you reach a small rest area on the left, complete with a water fountain, trash can, and kiosk—make note of the historical information and the bird-watching guide on the placards, and then continue on whenever you're ready. From here the trail opens onto a large, grassy knoll, with embankments rising on all sides. Continue north and east, and eventually cliffs and forest will close back in. As you hike, take advantage of the benches placed at regular intervals; while the trail is by no means strenuous, this area gets quite hot and dry during the summer.

Almost 1.3 miles from the trailhead, you pass under a railroad bridge. Note the artifacts of the trail's past history as a rail line: a network of wooden pylons, with cables linked to bolts drilled directly into the rock. These pylons and cables provide reinforcement to the surrounding rock, securing weak spots in case of potential rockslides. Resist the temptation to climb the pylons—they exist as a safety measure and are not to be used for horseplay.

Columbia Plateau State Park Trail:
Cheney Trailhead to Fish Lake

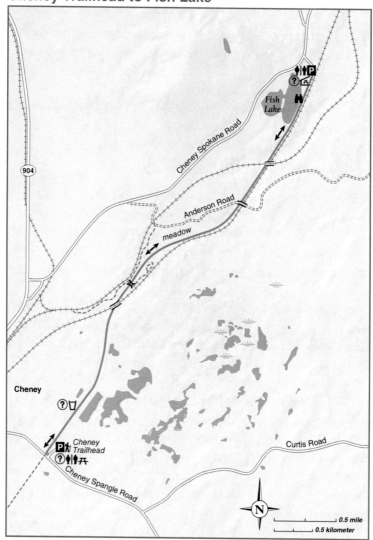

Just shy of 1.5 miles from the trailhead, you pass under a footbridge, and the dense forest cover continues for about 0.5 mile, after which point the trail opens onto a vast, open meadow. Here hikers are treated to a sweeping, pastoral view encompassing cabins, prairie grass, and a view of the nearby hills just to the west. Feel free to snap a few photos, but be mindful of cyclists coming and going. Note as well the deep, well-kept drainages to either side of the trail inside—in addition to helping keep your feet dry, they're also home to a host of wetland flora and fauna. The open section of the trail continues for roughly 0.75 mile before reverting to mixed woodland. The trail passes underneath Anderson Road at 2.6 miles and then a second railroad bridge at 2.9 miles.

About 0.5 mile past the second railway underpass, you'll come to one of the visual highlights of the trail: a scenic overlook on your left with a view of Fish Lake. Created thousands of years ago by massive floods, this body of water represents a striking piece of local geological history. According to the accompanying educational displays, a massive glacier in Northern Idaho failed at the end of the last glacial period, sending forth a rush of water measured in cubic miles, devastating everything in its path. Measuring hundreds of feet deep and moving at highway speeds, these floods lasted for days or weeks and occurred several times as ice dams formed and then receded again. Over time, the resulting erosion created the biome known today as the Channeled Scablands: a network of plateaus and canyons through which ancient floodwaters once careened on toward the Pacific. Feel free to rest here by the lake and enjoy the view; when ready, continue on for the final leg before the turnaround.

As you approach the turnaround point, at 3.8 miles, you'll once again find the trail enclosed by dense stands of pine. Up ahead you'll notice a series of traffic barriers across the trail—these mark the Fish Lake Trailhead entrance, where you'll find another paved parking area complete with covered picnic tables, restrooms, and map displays. Remember to dispose of any trash, recyclables, or pet waste before turning around and returning to the Cheney Trailhead.

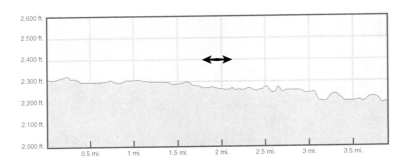

Nearby Attractions

This hike is close to a number of pleasant diversions, among them **Fish Lake.** Looking for more hiking? Check out **Turnbull National Wildlife Refuge** (see Hikes 4–6, pages 38, 42, and 47), or head over to nearby **Medical Lake,** which boasts a fantastic loop trail right in the heart of downtown (see Hike 3, page 34).

The sleepy university town of **Cheney** is home to a variety of family dining options, and the **Eastern Washington University** campus hosts numerous cultural events throughout the academic year.

Directions

From Monroe Street in downtown Spokane, drive westbound on I-90 for about 10 miles; then take Exit 270 and continue south 5.9 miles on WA 904/Lt. Michael P. Anderson Memorial Highway. In Cheney, turn left (southeast) onto F Street, which quickly becomes Mill Street and then South Cheney Spangle Road. In 0.8 mile, look for the paved parking area for the Cheney Trailhead on your left.

LOOKING OUT ACROSS THE PRAIRIE JUST SOUTH OF FISH LAKE

James T. Slavin Family Conservation Area Loop

SCENERY: ★ ★ ★ ★ ★
TRAIL CONDITION: ★ ★ ★ ★ ★
CHILDREN: ★
DIFFICULTY: ★
SOLITUDE: ★ ★ ★ ★ ★

OPEN GRASSLAND IN SLAVIN FAMILY CONSERVATION AREA

GPS TRAILHEAD COORDINATES: N47° 32.225' W117° 24.733'

DISTANCE & CONFIGURATION: 2.25-mile loop

HIKING TIME: 1 hour

HIGHLIGHTS: Views of Slavin Lake and surrounding wetlands, excellent bird-watching; secluded yet close to town

ELEVATION: 2,317' at lowest point, 2,417' at highest

ACCESS: Daily, sunrise–sunset; no fees or permits

MAPS: USGS *Spokane SW*; trail map at the website below and at trailhead

FACILITIES: Portable toilet, map board, and paved parking area at trailhead

WHEELCHAIR ACCESS: No

COMMENTS: This trail is popular with horseback riders, so be mindful of trail etiquette and yield where appropriate. Avoid approaching animals without riders' express permission, and remember to keep pets leashed.

CONTACTS: 509-477-4730, tinyurl.com/slavinconservationarea

James T. Slavin Family Conservation Area Loop

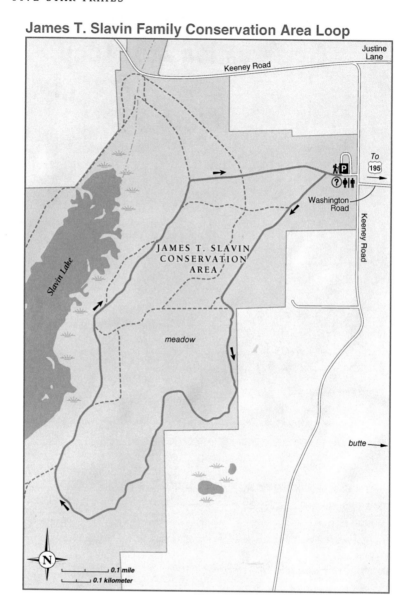

Overview

Located due south of Spokane, not far from the city of Marshall, this hike takes you through a broad swath of forests and wetlands, straddling the line between the Palouse grasslands to the south and the Channeled Scablands to the west.

This brief, gentle hike with a variety of gorgeous scenery is perfect for hikers of all ages and ability levels.

Route Details

Begin this hike from the paved parking area at the conservation area's eastern end. Note the large white farmhouse back across this road—this will be an important visual marker later. Bear in mind that this lot also serves as a staging area for horseback riders, so equestrian trailers will be a common sight. Give any horses a wide berth, and proceed straight ahead (west) down the trail after taking a moment to get your bearings at the map board.

There are numerous turns and junctions along this route, so make sure to consult this guide and stop frequently to reorient. To start, there will be a fork in the road about 300 feet from the trailhead—for the purposes of this hike, go left (southwest). Save the best views for last!

In a little more than 0.1 mile, you reach a junction with a trail heading right—bear left to continue south and west as the terrain begins to rise; before long, you'll find yourself in a wooded area, surrounded by pines.

One of the best parts of this hike is the relative silence to be found on the trail. Though set amid farms and rolling hills, on an average weekend day this trail is positively serene. Take a moment to appreciate the sounds of birdsong and of the wind in the grasses, though, as always, you should refrain from wandering off-trail; this not only helps preserve the local plant life but also helps you avoid common nuisances like ticks.

The journey through the initial leg will be reasonably straight, though the elevation will increase quickly. Don't be fooled by the aggressiveness of the

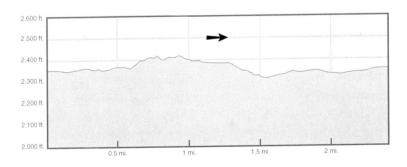

COMING TO THE FIRST RISE IN THE TRAIL

grade—this is just one of several very brief rises, so just focus on your pacing, stay hydrated, and don't feel compelled to rush. The payoff will be well worth it for the views alone.

About 0.4 mile from the trailhead, you reach another intersection with a trail heading right—keep left to stay on the main route. Follow the trail south and west over a series of rocky escarpments before curving north; in about 0.3 mile, arrive at the top of a large butte that affords a dramatic view of Slavin Lake to your west. Take a few pictures before moving on.

From the butte, the middle third of this hike veers south and west again, taking visitors above the treeline and over a series of cliffs composed of the same volcanic basalt common across much of this region. As you hike, you'll continue to encounter various grassy meadows, along with numerous stands of pine and fir. At about 1.1 miles along the trail, the path curves right (north), and about 0.3 mile farther, you reach another trail junction—keep straight where the other trail heads left. Then, about 0.1 mile ahead, pass another junction to your right. To the left, looking west, you can also see Slavin Lake and its surrounding wetlands. As is the case in much of the Channeled Scablands region, the underlying bedrock doesn't drain well, leading to the creation of numerous lakes and ponds, even at higher altitudes.

These wetlands provide a home for numerous species of birds, ranging from swallows all the way up to herons and sandhill cranes, each of which occupies a specific niche within the larger ecology. If ever you need a reminder of the interconnectedness of all living systems, look to the rivers and wetlands just beyond your back door.

At about 1.6 miles into the hike, just past another junction to your right, the trail curves right and then descends gradually over the next 0.6 mile. Along the way you'll pass two more junctions: keep to the right at both. By now you're heading northeast and skirting the eastern edge of Slavin Lake. Here again you'll find some wonderful opportunities for photography, as well as a chance to simply pause and take in the scenery. Bird-watchers would be well served to bring along a field guide, as this is a great spot to view wildlife without causing a disturbance.

The forest and grasslands give way to prairie once again, and for a few hundred yards past the last junction, the trail continues in ramrod-straight fashion. Note in the distance a pair of lone trees standing sentinel amid the fields. Not far past these, at about 2 miles into the hike, the trail hooks sharply right (east)—from here the scenery should quickly become familiar. In the distance, you should be able to make out the farmhouse from the beginning of the hike; use this to orient yourself as you cross the small rise through the grasses. You arrive back at the trailhead in a little more than 2.2 miles.

Directions

From Monroe Street in downtown Spokane, drive westbound on I-90 for about 0.9 mile; then take Exit 279 onto WA 195 South toward Colfax/Pullman. Follow WA 195 for roughly 8.5 miles; then turn right (west) onto East Washington Road. After 0.5 mile, take an immediate right onto South Keeney Road. The parking area will be just across the road on the left.

Medical Lake Loop

SCENERY: ★ ★ ★ ★
TRAIL CONDITION: ★ ★ ★ ★ ★
CHILDREN: ★ ★ ★ ★ ★
DIFFICULTY: ★
SOLITUDE: ★ ★ ★

MEDICAL LAKE VISTA FROM DUFFY'S POINT

GPS TRAILHEAD COORDINATES: N47° 34.675' W117° 41.540'

DISTANCE & CONFIGURATION: 3.0-mile loop

HIKING TIME: 1.25 hours

HIGHLIGHTS: Peaceful lake views, extensive forest cover, access to several parks along the route

ELEVATION: 2,396' at lowest point, 2,434' at highest

ACCESS: Open 24/7; no fees or permits

MAPS: USGS *Medical Lake, WA;* cp.spokanecounty.org/scout/map

FACILITIES: Restrooms, picnic benches, and paved parking at trailhead; numerous rest stops along the trail

WHEELCHAIR ACCESS: Yes

COMMENTS: Dogs must be leashed

CONTACTS: City of Medical Lake Parks and Trails, 509-565-5007, medical-lake.org/parks-trails; Spokane County Parks, Recreation & Golf, 509-477-4730, spokanecounty.org/1383/parks

Overview

This well-paved, gently graded loop winds through and around the town and lake of the same name. It's perfect for families with children as well as older and disabled hikers; plus, it boasts ready fishing access as well as numerous benches and rest areas. The local lake is named for the purported therapeutic properties of its mineral-rich waters, but even if you don't care to swim, the views of the water, numerous parks, and extensive tree cover are sure to be a balm for the spirit.

Route Details

Begin at the Medical Lake Access North Trailhead, at the far northern end of the lake. In the parking area, make note of the historical placard that details the park's history as a popular local recreation spot dating back to the 19th century. If you're interested in fishing, pay heed to the notice put up by the Washington Department of Fish & Wildlife, which lays out specific regulations regarding the use of fly lures.

If you've brought along your dog, please keep it leashed and under control, and avail yourself of the waste bags provided—even though this route lies close to town, a pack-in/pack-out ethos is still solid trail etiquette. Every hiker shares an obligation to keep these outdoor spaces beautiful for others.

From the parking area, the paved trail winds south, following the western lakeshore through dense stands of pine and fir. Springtime hikers may be lucky enough to spot wildflowers amid the undergrowth, so have a camera and a plant guide ready. As you make your way south, you'll notice a striking view to the right of a rock formation overhead—this marks the edge of the Eastern State Hospital grounds and forms the boundary between the cities of Medical Lake and West Medical Lake.

Continuing south, you come to a rest stop off to the left in 0.5 mile. This marks Duffy's Point, named for local resident Vincent "Duffy" Ready III, who passed away in 2016. His family dedicated a memorial bench where weary walkers can pause for a bit to gather themselves and enjoy a little peace and quiet overlooking the water. When you're ready, return to the trail.

The path stretches south for another 0.5 mile and then opens onto a vast clearing: this is Waterfront Park, one of the town's popular recreational spots. Head south past the baseball diamond off to the right, making note of the picnic

Medical Lake Loop

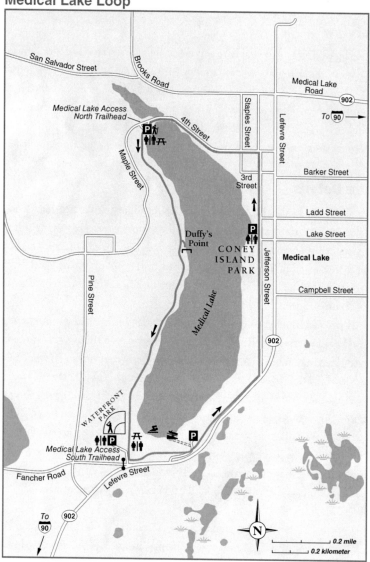

tables and grills near the water's edge—for day trippers in town with family, this represents a potentially ideal spot for a picnic or a swim. Otherwise, keep following the trail south and over the rise; then take a left at South Lefevre Street, heading east.

From here, the trail parallels Lefevre Street for a little more than 0.3 mile. Before long you'll arrive at the Medical Lake Access South Trailhead, which affords still more paved parking as well as restrooms, picnic areas, and a public boat launch. Continue another 0.3 mile, following Lefevre Street as it curves left; then take another left onto South Jefferson Street, and follow it north for the next 0.7 mile.

The pines and park lawns soon transition to sleepy residential areas, giving you a feel for the town of Medical Lake itself. As a precaution, keep left to follow the designated bike/pedestrian trail—there's no sidewalk for most of this section, and you'll be sharing the road with local vehicle traffic. If you're so inclined, feel free to detour into Coney Island Park, roughly halfway through this section. Take some time to relax on the green, well-manicured lawn; then continue north when ready.

When Jefferson reaches Fourth Street, take a left. In about 0.2 mile, the trail draws close to the lake again, and you enter the final stretch of this hike. By now the parking area where you began should be in sight. As the trail curves around, Fourth Street turns into Maple Street, and you reach your point of origin, closing the 3-mile loop. Remember, as always, to dispose of any animal waste or picnic trash—and congratulate yourself on a successful hike!

Nearby Attractions

Waterfront and **Coney Island Parks** are accessible directly from the trail. Also check out nearby **Turnbull National Wildlife Refuge**, the site of the next three hikes.

Directions

From Monroe Street in downtown Spokane, drive westbound on I-90 for about 7 miles; then take Exit 272 toward WA 902 West and Medical Lake. In 0.2 mile, bear right at the fork; then, in 0.1 mile, take the second exit off the traffic circle to continue west on WA 902. In 1.9 miles, proceed straight through a second traffic circle and continue west on WA 902; then, in 3.7 miles, WA 902 becomes Brooks Road after it crosses Lefevre Street. In 0.3 mile, turn left (south) onto North Howard Street; then, in 0.1 mile take the second right onto Fourth Street. Finally, 0.2 mile farther, turn left into the parking area for the Medical Lake Access North Trailhead.

4 Turnbull National Wildlife Refuge: Blackhorse Lake Trail

SCENERY: ★ ★ ★
TRAIL CONDITION: ★ ★ ★
CHILDREN: ★ ★ ★ ★ ★
DIFFICULTY: ★
SOLITUDE: ★ ★ ★

PAUSING AT THE SHORE ALONG THE BLACKHORSE LAKE TRAIL

GPS TRAILHEAD COORDINATES: N47° 25.396' W117° 32.391'

DISTANCE & CONFIGURATION: 0.7-mile balloon

HIKING TIME: 25 minutes

HIGHLIGHTS: Lake views, excellent bird-watching; a good choice if you're pressed for time

ELEVATION: 2,264' at lowest point, 2,282' at highest

ACCESS: Daily, sunrise–sunset; parking permit required March–October ($3/car or $3/family if walking or bicycling)

MAPS: USGS *Cheney, WA;* fws.gov/refuge/turnbull/map.html

FACILITIES: Restrooms, picnic pavilion, and paved parking at trailhead

WHEELCHAIR ACCESS: No

COMMENTS: The unpaved trail is muddy during spring and fall. While good for kids and navigable with trekking poles, this route is not recommended for those with disabilities. Dogs must be leashed.

CONTACTS: Turnbull National Wildlife Refuge, 509-235-4723, fws.gov/refuge/turnbull

Overview

Located within Turnbull National Wildlife Refuge just southwest of Cheney, this trail is somewhat out of the way but is a lovely spot for a picnic or a walk with dogs (leashed, of course). As with other trails in the Turnbull network, this is a great place for bird-watching—and unlike some other routes in the refuge, it's lightly trafficked, making it ideal for solitude seekers.

Route Details

Clearly marked by an orange sign, the Blackhorse Lake Trailhead is about 30 yards north of the parking lot on the west side of the Pine Creek Auto Tour Route. Per the aforementioned sign, bicycle traffic is prohibited (though given the marshy nature of this trail, that should be obvious).

Within the first few dozen yards, you come to a small footbridge, with a small pond off to your right and Blackhorse Lake beyond that. This footbridge doubles as a drainage that helps to protect the local ecosystem from sudden changes in water levels. Feel free to stop and catch a few photos, but be mindful of the warning placards and don't disturb the observation equipment. When ready, continue down the trail.

The soft, marshy soil here is composed largely of peat and sandy loam, so wear appropriate shoes as dictated by the weather. About 40 yards past the bridge, the trail reaches a bend; here you'll find a few picnic tables if you wish to bird-watch or simply take a load off. When you're ready to proceed, follow the curve of the trail left (south), and when it forks, a little more than 0.1 mile from the trailhead, take a right.

Throughout this hike, you should be able to see the parking area—don't expect much tree cover here, or wild changes in elevation. Where the trail *does* distinguish itself is its large, open clearings, which are perfect for photography and wildlife enthusiasts. Hikers with dogs may be tempted to unleash them so they can burn off a little energy, but park regulations expressly prohibit this. Dogs and the local ecology mix poorly, particularly when it comes to bird and rodent populations.

From the intersection marking the start of the loop, the trail winds south about 0.1 mile before curving east along the edges of the clearing; at this point the terrain rises slightly. This section of the clearing is ideal for picnics, but

Turnbull National Wildlife Refuge: Blackhorse Lake Trail

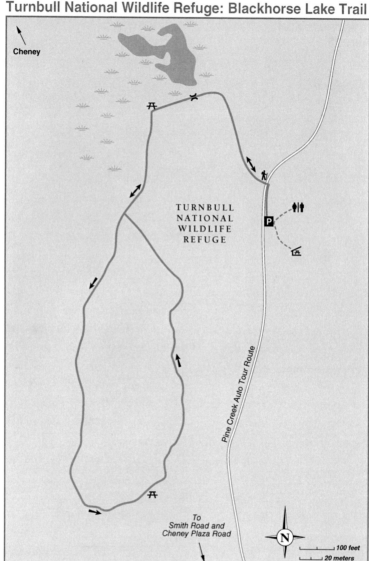

remember to pack out your trash. Also note that campfires are prohibited—the wildlife area is extremely prone to brushfires in summer.

Past another picnic area on your right at 0.3 mile, the trail winds back north again, and the surroundings should become increasingly familiar. In another 0.2 mile, go right at the fork to close the loop; then hang a right past the picnic tables, and head back over the footbridge to the trailhead.

Nearby Attractions

See the next two hikes for more opportunities to explore Turnbull National Wildlife Refuge. Additionally, check out the nearby refuge headquarters for educational resources. And when you're done hiking, you can swing through Cheney or into Spokane to explore the diverse dining and cultural options.

Directions

From Monroe Street in downtown Spokane, drive westbound on I-90 for about 10 miles; then take Exit 270 onto WA 904 West toward Four Lakes/Cheney. Follow WA 904 for an additional 6.3 miles, continuing through downtown Cheney; then turn left (south) onto South Cheney Plaza Road. In 4.2 miles, turn left (southeast) onto South Smith Road. Continue 1.8 miles, passing the Smith Road parking area on your left; then bear left (north) at the fork, then left again at another fork in 0.1 mile. In 0.6 mile, the parking area will be on your right.

ROUNDING THE FIRST BEND ON THE TRAIL

5

Turnbull National Wildlife
Refuge: Pine Lake—Headquarters Loop

SCENERY: ★ ★ ★
TRAIL CONDITION: ★ ★ ★ ★ ★
CHILDREN: ★ ★ ★ ★ ★
DIFFICULTY: ★
SOLITUDE: ★ ★

MIDDLE PINE LAKE IN TURNBULL NATIONAL WILDLIFE REFUGE

GPS TRAILHEAD COORDINATES: N47° 24.889' W117° 32.279'

DISTANCE & CONFIGURATION: 1.6-mile loop

HIKING TIME: 75 minutes

HIGHLIGHTS: Excellent for wildlife watchers and those with disabilities; numerous informational exhibits

ELEVATION: 2,229' at lowest point, 2,283' at highest

ACCESS: Daily, 6 a.m.–8 p.m.; parking permit required March–October ($3/car or $3/family if walking or bicycling)

MAPS: USGS *Cheney, WA;* fws.gov/refuge/turnbull/map.html

FACILITIES: Restrooms and paved parking at trailhead; additional parking and restrooms at refuge headquarters

WHEELCHAIR ACCESS: Yes

COMMENTS: Dogs must be leashed

CONTACTS: Turnbull National Wildlife Refuge, 509-235-4723, fws.gov/refuge/turnbull

Overview

This trail in Turnbull National Wildlife Refuge sits at the confluence of Spokane's three major biomes: mixed pine forest, the Palouse steppe, and the Channeled Scablands, with wetland preserves dominating the refuge itself. As a result, this is a prime spot for bird-watchers, as well as for families and anyone looking for an easy, relaxed hike. Bring binoculars and a birding guide.

Route Details

This hike uses sections of two trails—the Pine Lake Loop Trail (see next hike) and the Headquarters Trail—to form a large loop, and it begins from the same parking area as the one for the Pine Lake Loop Trail.

The trailhead lies directly south of and across Smith Road from the east side of the parking area—look for the information kiosk before you cross the road—and is paved from the outset. Pay attention to the signage indicating that bicycles are strictly prohibited, and make note as well of the viewfinders and a bench just off to the right. This is a great spot to pause for a prehike snack, get your bearings, or otherwise to observe the lakes and local wildlife from a distance. When you're ready, head on down the trail.

At first the trail follows a potentially confusing S-curve on its way down to the lakeshore. Don't be deterred, though—just keep following the paved surface. When you reach a trail junction less than 0.1 mile from the parking area, turn right (southwest).

The path affords panoramic views of Winslow Pool to your left, along with the surrounding wetlands that border them. To your right are grassy slopes and stands of pine, along with isolated stretches of cattail pond. Pay close attention to the ground as you walk, as birds aren't the only creatures that call this area home—careful hikers may spy ground squirrels, muskrats, and garter snakes moving through the brush. Mind the goose droppings!

About 0.2 mile from the previous trail junction, you'll see a small stone monument on your left. It bears a dedication in honor of Winslow Pool's namesake, Ralph O. Winslow, who managed the refuge in the years following World War II. A few yards past the memorial marker, you reach a bench on your left and another junction marking the start of the loop. The trail to the left leads to a small footbridge that divides Winslow Pool from Middle Pine Lake and also

Turnbull National Wildlife Refuge: Pine Lake–Headquarters Loop

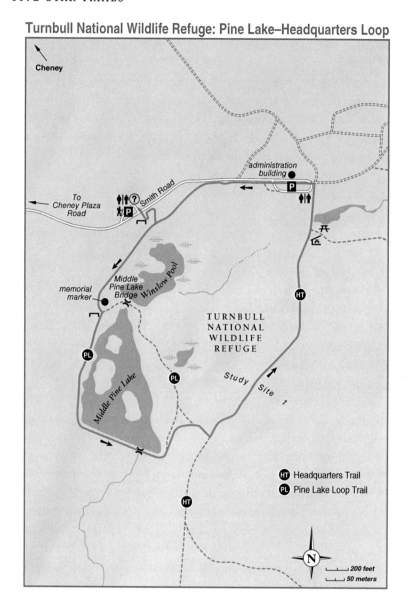

serves as a drainage channel between them. This bridge forms part of the return leg for the Pine Lake Loop Trail (see next hike), but for this hike you continue right, down along the main path.

The trail winds south and then east, hewing close to the shore of Middle Pine Lake. At a little more than 0.5 mile into the hike, you come to a footbridge that doubles as a drainage channel for the local ecosystem. Note the observation platforms, as well as the official notices warning visitors away. In addition to helping keep visitors' feet dry, the culverts here help keep water circulating throughout the wetlands, thus preserving habitat for the area's resident waterfowl and plant life. Compared with many other ecosystems, wetlands are incredibly fragile and susceptible to disruption, so it's important to respect both the land and the structures put in place to help preserve it. After stopping to snap a few photos and take in the views, continue southeast along the lakeshore.

In 0.1 mile, the trail curves north again, bringing you to a junction with a spur for the Headquarters Trail—turn right and, in another 0.1 mile, turn left at another junction to continue on the Headquarters Trail. There may be a brief patch on the spur where the path is washed out, but aside from a few puddles, the inconvenience should be minimal. After about 50 yards, the elevation rises and conditions return to normal.

The trail heads northeast, away from the lakes and into coniferous woodland. The soil becomes grassy and dry here, so feel free to wander a bit farther

WOODLANDS, PRAIRIES, AND WETLANDS COEXIST IN THIS SCENIC WILDLIFE REFUGE.

afield. One exception is denoted by signs indicating Study Site 1, a wilderness research area used by the biology department at nearby Eastern Washington University. Again, please be considerate, and don't disturb the observation platforms and equipment.

A little more than 1 mile into the hike, you pass a trail junction and picnic area on your right—keep heading straight (north). About 0.1 mile ahead, you'll come to the refuge's administration building, on your left just before Smith Road; here, you can peruse official literature as well as view informational exhibits. The administration building also hosts the return segment of this hike—to find it, look for the gravel path behind and to the west of the administration building, and head straight (west), with Smith Road to your right (north).

After about 0.1 mile, the trail begins to curve left (southwest), and you'll soon notice viewfinders and a log bench on the hill to your right, marking the junction that leads to the Pine Lake Loop Trailhead. In another 0.1 mile, turn right, proceed back up the paved switchback, and cross Smith Road to return to the parking area.

Nearby Attractions

See the previous and next hikes for more opportunities to explore Turnbull National Wildlife Refuge; also check out fws.gov/refuge/turnbull for information on trails not covered here. After your hike, you can head back into Cheney for a bite to eat or check out one of the many cultural events being presented at Eastern Washington University. The varied trail options, coupled with the refuge's proximity to a college town, make for a wealth of recreational opportunities for every taste.

Directions

From Monroe Street in downtown Spokane, drive westbound on I-90 for about 10 miles; then take Exit 270 onto WA 904 West toward Four Lakes/Cheney. Follow WA 904 for an additional 6.3 miles, continuing through downtown Cheney; then turn left (south) onto South Cheney Plaza Road. In 4.2 miles, turn left (southeast) onto South Smith Road. In 1.5 miles, the parking area will be on your left.

6

Turnbull National Wildlife Refuge: Pine Lake Loop Trail

SCENERY: ★ ★ ★
TRAIL CONDITION: ★ ★ ★ ★ ★
CHILDREN: ★ ★ ★ ★ ★
DIFFICULTY: ★
SOLITUDE: ★ ★

WINSLOW POOL   photographed by Elizabeth Marlin

GPS TRAILHEAD COORDINATES: N47° 24.889' W117° 32.279'

DISTANCE & CONFIGURATION: 1.2-mile balloon

HIKING TIME: 30 minutes

HIGHLIGHTS: Excellent for bird-watching and those with disabilities

ELEVATION: 2,229' at lowest point, 2,253' at highest

ACCESS: Daily, 6 a.m.–8 p.m.; parking permit required March–October ($3/car or $3/family if walking or bicycling)

MAPS: USGS *Cheney, WA;* fws.gov/refuge/turnbull/map.html

FACILITIES: Restrooms, information kiosk, observation post, and paved parking at trailhead

WHEELCHAIR ACCESS: Yes

COMMENTS: Dogs must be leashed

CONTACTS: Turnbull National Wildlife Refuge, 509-235-4723, fws.gov/refuge/turnbull

Turnbull National Wildlife Refuge: Pine Lake Loop Trail

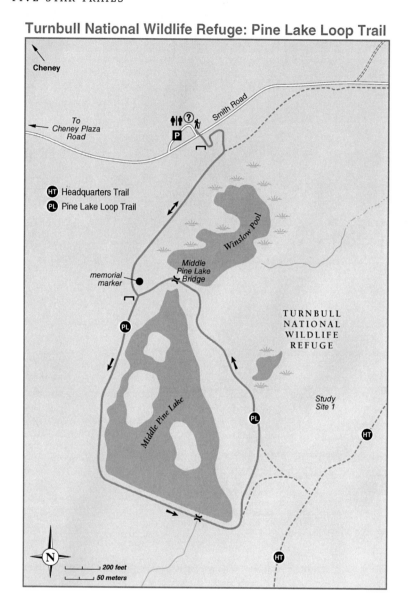

Cheney

To
Cheney Plaza
Road

Smith Road

HT Headquarters Trail
PL Pine Lake Loop Trail

Winslow Pool

memorial
marker

Middle
Pine Lake
Bridge

PL

TURNBULL
NATIONAL
WILDLIFE
REFUGE

Middle Pine Lake

PL

Study
Site 1

HT

HT

N

200 feet
50 meters

Overview

Located a 30-minute drive southwest of Spokane, this trail in Turnbull National Wildlife Refuge takes in both Winslow Pool and Middle Pine Lake; it features footbridges as well as rest areas and scenic overlooks. Its gentle grade and paved surfaces make it a perfect fit for older and disabled visitors, as well as for families with children. Opportunities to observe local wildlife abound.

Route Details

The trailhead lies directly south of and across Smith Road from the east side of the parking area—look for the information kiosk before you cross the road—and is paved from the outset. Pay attention to the signage indicating that bicycles are strictly prohibited, and make note as well of the viewfinders and a bench just off to the right. This is a great spot to pause for a prehike snack, get your bearings, or otherwise to observe the lakes and local wildlife from a distance. When you're ready, head on down the trail.

At first the trail follows a potentially confusing S-curve on its way down to the lakeshore. Don't be deterred, though—just keep following the paved surface. When you reach a trail junction less than 0.1 mile from the parking area, turn right (southwest).

The path affords panoramic views of Winslow Pool to your left, along with the surrounding wetlands that border them. To your right are grassy slopes and stands of pine, along with isolated stretches of cattail pond. Pay close attention to the ground as you walk, as birds aren't the only creatures that call this area home—careful hikers may spy ground squirrels, muskrats, and garter snakes moving through the brush. Mind the goose droppings!

About 0.1 mile from the previous trail junction, you'll see a small stone monument on your left. It bears a dedication in honor of Winslow Pool's namesake, Ralph O. Winslow, who managed the refuge in the years following World War II. A few yards past the memorial marker, you reach a bench on your left and another junction marking the start of the loop. It may be tempting to take the left over the Middle Lake Bridge, but that's part of your return leg, so for this hike, you continue right.

The trail winds south and then east, hewing close to the shore of Middle Pine Lake. Again, keep an eye out for frequent goose droppings in addition to more-pleasant sightings of waterfowl and other wildlife. At a little more than 0.5 mile into the hike, you come to a footbridge that doubles as a drainage channel for the local ecosystem. Pay special attention to the vista stretching off to the south, which shows off the local wetlands in all of their full, sprawling glory.

This also makes for a fantastic spot to snap a few photos, but please stay off the marked platform, which is for staff only. After you've had your fill of the views, continue on the path.

In another 0.1 mile, the lakeshore curves north again, bringing you to a junction with a spur for the Headquarters Trail (see previous hike) and then another spur junction 0.1 mile ahead—keep left at both forks. The trail traces the eastern shore of Middle Pine Lake as it proceeds north into a large stand of ponderosa pine; here, however, the trail doesn't trace the lake as closely as the stretch along the western shore. Rounding a bend at a little more than 0.75 mile into the hike, you'll come upon signage marking a small pond to the right. Remember, as always, to stay on the official paths—the local watershed is poorly suited to swimming and other aquatic recreation. Take a few minutes to enjoy the scenery.

A few yards past the pond, you'll emerge from the woods and pass a small clearing on the left (west) with scenic views, but heed the signage: this area is a foraging site for local fowl, marked BIRDS ONLY BEYOND THIS POINT. Beyond providing outdoor access and educational opportunities to the public, the primary mission of Turnbull Wildlife Refuge is conservation, so please be considerate and don't venture off the trail.

Past the clearing, the trail rises slightly, staying close to a grassy escarpment to the right. The terrain here represents a striking microcosm of the geography common to much of the Channeled Scablands biome. Created by a combination of volcanic activity and mass flooding at the end of the last glacial period, the rocks here present a millennia-old record of the region's geological history—yet another reminder of the importance of the conservation efforts underway at Turnbull, and of humanity's comparatively swift impact on the local ecology.

Continue on the trail, now heading northwest, and after almost 1 mile of hiking, you should recognize a familiar landmark: the Middle Pine Lake Bridge. Pause for a few photos; then turn right at the intersection to close the loop, and finally head back up and around the S-curve and across Smith Road to return to the parking area.

Nearby Attractions

See the previous two hikes for more opportunities to explore Turnbull National Wildlife Refuge. Additionally, the refuge headquarters contains educational displays and access to other resources for the curious. The college town of Cheney, just a few miles up the road, serves up not only a variety of dining options but also an ever-changing roster of sporting and cultural events at Eastern Washington University.

Directions

From Monroe Street in downtown Spokane, drive westbound on I-90 for about 10 miles; then take Exit 270 onto WA 904 West toward Four Lakes/Cheney. Follow WA 904 for an additional 6.3 miles, continuing through downtown Cheney; then turn left (south) onto South Cheney Plaza Road. In 4.2 miles, turn left (southeast) onto South Smith Road. In 1.5 miles, the parking area will be on your left.

NOT JUST WILDLIFE: THE REFUGE IS ALSO HOME TO ABUNDANT SEASONAL WILDFLOWERS.
photographed by Elizabeth Marlin

West Spokane

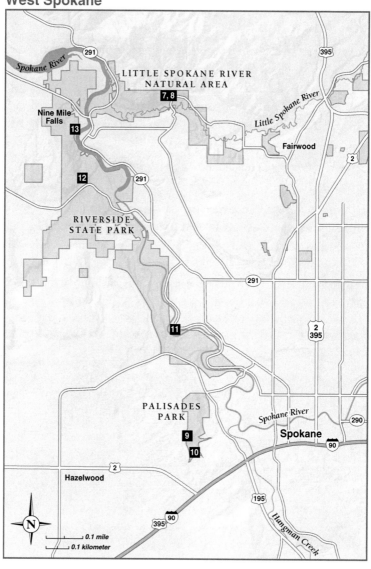

West Spokane

CENTENNIAL TRAIL SHORELINE IN RIVERSIDE STATE PARK (SEE HIKE 13, PAGE 84)

photographed by Elizabeth Marlin

7

Little Spokane River Natural Area: Indian Painted Rocks and Knothead Valley Loop

NEAR THE SUMMIT ON THE KNOTHEAD VALLEY LOOP

SCENERY: ★ ★ ★ ★
TRAIL CONDITION: ★ ★ ★ ★ ★
CHILDREN: ★ ★ ★
DIFFICULTY: ★ ★ ★
SOLITUDE: ★ ★ ★ ★ ★

GPS TRAILHEAD COORDINATES: N47° 46.955' W117° 29.814'

DISTANCE & CONFIGURATION: 6.5-mile loop

HIKING TIME: 2.75 hours

HIGHLIGHTS: Views of the Little Spokane River, Long Lake, and Knothead Valley; excellent wildlife-viewing

ELEVATION: 1,551' at lowest point, 2,462' at highest

ACCESS: Daily, 8 a.m.–sunset in winter, 6:30 a.m.–sunset in summer; best accessed late spring–early fall. A Washington State Parks Discover Pass ($10/day, $30/year) is required for parking.

MAPS: USGS *Nine Mile Falls, WA;* maps.spokanecity.org and at trailhead

FACILITIES: Restrooms, trash can, map board, and gravel parking lot at trailhead

WHEELCHAIR ACCESS: No

COMMENTS: Dogs and cyclists are prohibited in this natural area. The southern end of the loop is prone to flooding, given its proximity to the river.

CONTACTS: Riverside State Park, 509-465-5064, parks.state.wa.us/573/riverside; Spokane County Parks, Recreation & Golf, 509-477-4730, spokanecounty.org/1383/parks

Overview

This hike in the Little Spokane River Natural Area, a protected section within Riverside State Park, takes you through pristine wetlands before winding through rugged evergreen slopes. Its proximity to the Little Spokane River makes it a prime spot for both kayakers and bird-watchers, and the trail's upper reaches are home to large numbers of white-tailed and mule deer.

Route Details

The Indian Painted Rocks Trailhead is easily identified by its namesake rock formation, to the right (east) of the parking area. From the west side of the parking area, directly opposite the restrooms, head straight (west) past a brown trailhead sign to your left and a map board to your right.

The initial leg consists of an east–west straightaway with only minor changes in elevation. (See the next hike for a more in-depth description of this section.) The path here is bordered on the left by extensive wetlands. Kayakers will find much to enjoy here, and bird-watchers will find much to see, as this area is home to large populations of mallard ducks and American coots; sightings of ospreys and herons are also quite common. As a reminder, please don't feed the wildlife—this disrupts the animals' natural feeding patterns and can potentially harm the local watershed. As always, responsible conservation starts with the individual.

Note the granite cliffs off to your right; in addition to making for great photo opportunities, they present a great challenge for rock-climbing enthusiasts. The cliffs themselves are a good distance above the immediate trail itself, giving hikers and climbers plenty of space between them; nevertheless, be mindful of other visitors, and exercise appropriate courtesy. Additionally, beware of fallen logs through this area, as many trees show evidence of fire damage.

About 1.5 miles into the hike, the terrain begins to rise gradually, culminating in a sharp hairpin turn to the right a little more than 0.1 mile ahead. Follow this paved section, which marks the junction of the Indian Painted Rocks and Knothead Valley Trails, across River Park Lane; then take the unimproved trail up and to the left. From here, the trail follows a gentle S-curve, leading up through grassy slopes lightly studded with pine. White-tailed and mule deer are common sights, so have that camera ready.

Little Spokane River Natural Area:
Indian Painted Rocks and Knothead Valley Loop

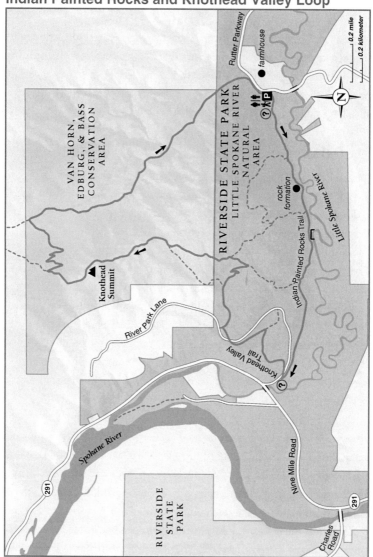

After a second hairpin turn—this time to the left and about 0.35 mile from the first—the climb becomes decidedly more rugged, and in about 0.25 mile, the trail crosses River Park Lane a second time. Please observe the signage in this area marking the boundaries between the state park and private property, and refrain from venturing off-trail. Continue across the road, following the dirt path generally east and passing two trail junctions to your left, at 2.3 miles and 2.6 miles, respectively. Then, a little more than 0.1 mile farther, you enter an S-curve switchback; about 0.2 mile after that, you reach a third trail junction—take a sharp left to head north.

Eventually, you'll find yourself ascending past the treeline. Make use of the view to capture a few shots of Long Lake off to the northwest, and note the Selkirk Mountains far to the north. Just shy of 3.8 miles into the hike, you reach Knothead Summit, the loop's high point (2,462'), to your left.

A little more than 0.3 mile past the summit, you pass another trail junction to the left and then enter a series of switchbacks; then, at yet another junction 0.6 mile ahead, make a sharp right, heading south. From here the descent begins, and the trail loops back toward home.

The trail is now much more consistent in grade. Given that this section lies along the northeast face of the Indian Painted Rocks, visitors should expect denser forest cover, as well as deeper snowfall and mud conditions depending on the season. Though the descent itself is gentle, the trail narrows, so tread slowly and wear appropriate hiking shoes/boots—no sense in risking an ankle injury so close to the end of the hike.

At a little more than 6.2 miles into the hike, you'll intersect a footpath that follows Rutter Parkway, with a farmhouse visible just across the road. Though this area may look unfamiliar, it's only about 0.1 mile from where the trail began. Head right, and be mindful of the clear-cuts. Before long, the parking area will come into view.

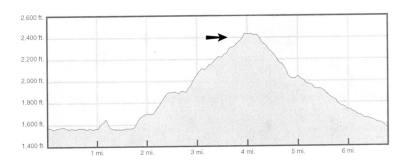

Nearby Attractions

This hike lies within **Riverside State Park,** which offers plentiful opportunities for camping, fishing, swimming, and of course hiking (see Hikes 11–13, pages 73, 78, and 84). Also check out nearby **Palisades Park** (see Hikes 9 and 10, pages 64 and 68) and **People's Park** for additional outdoor fun, or cool off at **Long Lake** when the mercury rises. And you're just a stone's throw away from the restaurants, nightlife, and shopping of downtown Spokane.

Directions

From Spokane, take I-90 westbound to Exit 280A for the Maple Street Bridge. At the end of the ramp, continue straight for one block on West Fourth Avenue; then turn right (north) onto North Walnut Street. In 0.2 mile (two blocks), bear slightly left to continue north on Walnut Street, which soon becomes North Maple Street; then, in about 0.4 mile, cross the Spokane River on the Maple Street Bridge. Continue north on Maple Street for 4.8 miles; then turn left (west) onto WA 291/West Francis Avenue. In 1.1 miles, bear right (northwest) onto West Indian Trail Road, and continue for 6 miles as Indian Trail turns into Rural Route 5/West Rutter Parkway. The trailhead parking area will be on your left, at the base of the Indian Painted Rocks.

HEADING WEST ON THE INDIAN PAINTED ROCKS TRAIL

8

Little Spokane River Natural
Area: Indian Painted Rocks Trail

SCENERY: ★ ★ ★ ★ ★
TRAIL CONDITION: ★ ★ ★ ★ ★
CHILDREN: ★ ★ ★ ★
DIFFICULTY: ★ ★
SOLITUDE: ★ ★

A VIEW OF THE LITTLE SPOKANE RIVER IN THE INDIAN PAINTED ROCKS AREA

GPS TRAILHEAD COORDINATES: N47° 46.955' W117° 29.814'

DISTANCE & CONFIGURATION: 1.7-mile out-and-back

HIKING TIME: 1.5 hours

HIGHLIGHTS: Views of Indian Painted Rock, Little Spokane River; ample opportunities for bird-watching

ELEVATION: 1,550' at lowest point, 1,650' at highest

ACCESS: Daily, 8 a.m.–sunset in winter, 6:30 a.m.–sunset in summer; best accessed late spring–early fall. A Washington State Parks Discover Pass ($10/day, $30/year) is required for parking.

MAPS: USGS *Nine Mile Falls, WA*; maps.spokanecity.org and at trailhead

FACILITIES: Restrooms, trash can, map board, and gravel parking lot at trailhead

WHEELCHAIR ACCESS: No

COMMENTS: Dogs and cyclists are prohibited in this natural area. The southern end of the loop is prone to flooding, given its proximity to the river.

Little Spokane River Natural Area: Indian Painted Rocks Trail

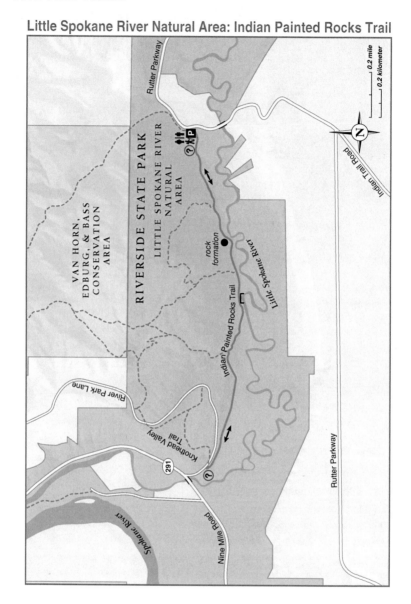

CONTACTS: Riverside State Park, 509-465-5064, parks.state.wa.us/573/riverside; Spokane County Parks, Recreation & Golf, 509-477-4730, spokanecounty.org/1383/parks

Overview

Located within the Little Spokane River Natural Area in Riverside State Park, this hike also comprises the initial leg of the Indian Painted Rocks–Knothead Valley Loop (see previous hike). The unpaved, moderately trafficked trail is good for families with older children. Trekking poles may come in handy for one particularly rocky spot, but for the most part this trail experiences minimal change in elevation.

Route Details

The Indian Painted Rocks Trailhead lies on the west side of the parking area, directly opposite the restrooms. Aim for a clear day when attempting this route, as inclement weather can obscure this hike's defining feature: the towering Indian Painted Rocks. Named for the painted figures adorning the rocks near the trailhead, this formation provides concrete evidence of early indigenous settlement in the region. Before setting out, feel free to examine these paintings, which are easily accessed from the parking lot and are clearly marked by a protective metal grate overhead. When ready, return to the trailhead and head straight (west) past a brown trailhead sign to your left and a map board to your right.

In addition to its proximity to town and relatively short duration, the primary appeal of this trail lies in the visual contrasts provided by its scenery. To the right (north) loom the Indian Painted Rocks, while to the left (south) lie the broad, flat shallows of the Little Spokane River. In spring and summer, you can witness the effects of soil erosion on the river's ever-shifting banks, with lazy waters snaking through lush, open meadows. This effect is a result of sediments deposited by the river, which serve to slow and eventually redirect the flow of the river itself. For more information, check the frequent signposts, six in all, that line this trail. Smartphone users can scan the accompanying QR codes for access to helpful educational supplements.

The initial 0.5 mile is hard packed and flat, proceeding generally west-southwest. At about 0.55 mile, you'll come to a small rock formation. The trail appears to dead-end but actually continues past this point, so climb over the rocks, minding your footing and taking care to maintain multiple points of contact. If you've brought trekking poles, this would be a prime spot to use them.

CRESTING THE FIRST RISE NEAR INDIAN PAINTED ROCKS

Once over the rocks, the trail rises slightly. Watch for logfalls in this area, and contact Spokane County Parks, Recreation & Golf (509-477-4730) to report any blockages. At the approximate halfway point for this hike, a little more than 0.8 mile in, you'll encounter a slight fork—take the path to the right, which not only boasts a small wooden bench, on the right at the top of the rise, but also conveniently avoids the washout down below on the left. Feel free to rest here, and continue when ready.

Up to this point, the trail has been generally straight and flat. That changes, however, not far past the bench, as you encounter a deep draw and a dry tributary streambed. Navigate this crossing and climb the switchbacks leading up the other side. Almost 1 mile into the hike, the trail rises again, diverging north and away from the river.

The terrain in this section skirts a high ridge well above the waterline, with an impressive view of the river valley. The grade may seem steep, but thankfully this section is only a few hundred yards, at which point the downhill slope opens onto a great view of Long Lake off to the northwest. The high vantage point provides a great lookout for photographers and bird-watchers, so be sure to catch a few shots and have those wildlife guides at the ready.

The final leg of this trail, about 1.25 miles in, hews to the edges of a vast clearing, bordered on the right by tall pines and on the left by fallow fields and marshland. Take some time to enjoy the pastoral aesthetic and stark visual contrasts on display. About 0.3 mile past the clearing, the trail bends to the right and begins to rise again, culminating in a map board and a road crossing. Here you can turn around or continue on the Indian Painted Rocks–Knothead Valley Loop, profiled previously.

Nearby Attractions

This hike lies within **Riverside State Park,** which offers plentiful opportunities for camping, fishing, swimming, and of course hiking (see Hikes 11–13, pages 73, 78, and 84). More hiking can be found at **Downriver Park** as well as **Palisades Park** (see Hikes 9 and 10, pages 64 and 68), both less than 10 minutes away. Finally, check out **Nine Mile Reservoir,** along with **Fort George Wright** and the adjacent **Military Cemetery.**

Directions

From Spokane, take I-90 westbound to Exit 280A for the Maple Street Bridge. At the end of the ramp, continue straight for one block on West Fourth Avenue; then turn right (north) onto North Walnut Street. In 0.2 mile (two blocks), bear slightly left to continue north on Walnut Street, which soon becomes North Maple Street; then, in about 0.4 mile, cross the Spokane River on the Maple Street Bridge. Continue north on Maple Street for 4.8 miles; then turn left (west) onto WA 291/West Francis Avenue. In 1.1 miles, bear right (northwest) onto West Indian Trail Road, and continue for 6 miles as Indian Trail turns into Rural Route 5/West Rutter Parkway. The trailhead parking area will be on your left, at the base of the Indian Painted Rocks.

Palisades Park: Upper Loop

SCENERY: ★ ★ ★ ★
TRAIL CONDITION: ★ ★ ★
CHILDREN: ★ ★ ★ ★ ★
DIFFICULTY: ★
SOLITUDE: ★

PALISADES PARK IS A QUIET OASIS A SHORT DRIVE FROM DOWNTOWN.

GPS TRAILHEAD COORDINATES: N47° 39.284' W117° 29.187'

DISTANCE & CONFIGURATION: 3.1-mile balloon

HIKING TIME: 1.15 hours

HIGHLIGHTS: Great forest hiking; views of Sunset Hill and the city of Spokane

ELEVATION: 2,164' at lowest point, 2,209' at highest

ACCESS: Daily, 6 a.m.–10 p.m.; no fees or permits

MAPS: USGS *Spokane NW, WA;* palisadesnw.com/palisades-map.html and at trailhead

FACILITIES: Map board and gravel parking lot at trailhead

WHEELCHAIR ACCESS: No

COMMENTS: The return leg of this hike is prone to minor flooding in springtime, so bring water-resistant footwear depending on the season; dogs must be leashed

CONTACTS: Spokane City Parks and Recreation, 509-625-6200, palisadesnw.com

Overview

Located in Palisades Park just west of Spokane, this hike traverses a high wooded plateau marking the boundary between West Spokane and the West Plains. It features a lengthy cliffside straightaway with numerous spots for impromptu picnicking, as well as a truly majestic view of Spokane. The loop is great for kids, dogs, and older hikers because of its gentle grade; plus, it's easily accessible from town. The corollary, of course, is that you can expect to encounter other visitors virtually year-round—those looking to escape the throngs will want to search farther afield.

Route Details

The trailhead for this hike is marked by a small gravel parking lot furnished with visitor information and a historical placard. Additional parking is available roughly 360 feet up the trail on the left. Walk around the locked gate adjacent to this parking area, and proceed northeast on the gravel path, listed on the park map as Rimrock Drive. In about 0.2 mile, you reach a junction with Trail 103, which heads left (northwest)—continue straight on Rimrock Drive, and then pass another junction with Trail 103, now to your right (east), 0.1 mile farther.

As you proceed north along the cliffside, it should quickly become obvious what makes this hike so popular with locals. Along the initial leg alone, hikers are afforded scenic views of Sunset Hill and the bustling skyline of downtown Spokane. From here, you can see Latah (also known as Hangman) Creek and People's Park off to the east and the town of Nine Mile Falls, about 13 miles to the north. On a clear day looking east, you can make out Beacon Hill, Micah Peak, and Mount Spokane.

Numerous scenic overlooks along the trail offer great photo opportunities. In addition to the views mentioned above, you can glance farther down and spy, amid the pines, a few of the signature basalt pillars for which this region is known. Feel free to rest anywhere along the side of the trail; numerous grassy knolls would make perfect spots for a picnic.

At almost 0.9 mile into the hike, you reach an intersection with Trail 101—continue straight (north) on Rimrock Drive. The trail then begins to arc north and west before moving into an area of ponderosa and spruce growth. About 0.4 mile past the previous intersection, you reach another one: here,

Palisades Park: Upper Loop

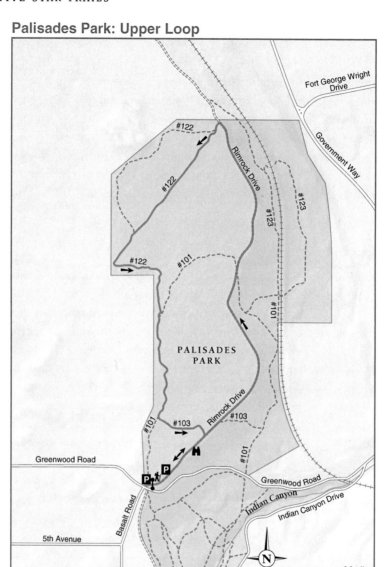

Rimrock Drive continues north and west—make a sharp left onto Trail 122, heading southwest. Just 150 feet farther, you pass a junction with a trail to your right, also labeled (rather confusingly) as Trail 122 on the park map.

Both the trail and the terrain change considerably in the second half of the loop. The geology here is distinguished by basalt substrate with layers of sandy soil and loam on top. This combination is ideal for the hardy ponderosa pine, but it also absorbs rainfall poorly, so expect large stretches of the track to become marshy in springtime, as the snowfall melts. Bring appropriate footwear for the season.

After following a small seasonal streambed on your left for about 0.5 mile from the last turn, you cross a small earthen berm, where, now 2 miles from the trailhead, Trail 122 hooks sharply left. Before long the tree growth encroaches on the trail, and the path itself grows narrower and more winding. The route bends gradually rightward until you enter a vast meadow studded by tall pines. This is another great place to rest, picnic, or snap photos. Linger a bit, then continue when ready.

The trail continues virtually due south. Springtime hikers will find that the path is muddy and slippery, so exercise caution, wear proper footwear, and use trekking poles if necessary.

The final 0.4 mile is marked by yet another fork—you can either keep straight (south) along Trail 101 or make a sharp left (east) onto Trail 103. While Trail 101 provides a more direct route back to the parking area, it isn't as well maintained as Trail 103; plus, it's subject to flooding. For this hike, then, make the left onto Trail 103, follow it 0.2 mile back to Rimrock Drive (the out-and-back "string" of this balloon loop), and turn right. Then proceed about 0.5 mile south and west, past the gate, to the trailhead parking area.

Directions

From Monroe Street in downtown Spokane, take I-90 westbound for about 2.4 miles; then take Exit 277 for US 2 West toward Davenport. After about 0.1 mile, get into the far right lane, signed for Garden Springs. Follow the hairpin curve; then, in 0.3 mile, turn left (north) onto South Rustle Road. In 0.1 mile, take another left onto West Sunset Boulevard, heading northwest. In 0.6 mile, turn right (north) onto South Basalt Street, and follow it for 0.9 mile. Just after you cross West Greenwood Road, look for a dirt parking pull-off on the left.

10 **Palisades Park:** Mystic Falls Loop

SCENERY: ★ ★ ★ ★
TRAIL CONDITION: ★ ★
CHILDREN: ★ ★ ★ ★
DIFFICULTY: ★ ★
SOLITUDE: ★

THE BASE OF MYSTIC FALLS

GPS TRAILHEAD COORDINATES: N47° 38.948' W117° 28.882'

DISTANCE & CONFIGURATION: 0.8-mile out-and-back/balloon

HIKING TIME: 30–45 minutes

HIGHLIGHTS: Waterfall at turnaround, 2 small caves

ELEVATION: 1,963' at lowest point, 2,089' at highest

ACCESS: Daily, 6 a.m.–10 p.m.; no fees or permits

MAPS: USGS *Spokane NW, WA*; palisadesnw.com/palisades-map.html and at trailhead

FACILITIES: Map board at trailhead

WHEELCHAIR ACCESS: No

COMMENTS: Be careful when crossing streams; dogs must be leashed.

CONTACTS: Spokane City Parks and Recreation, 509-625-6200, palisadesnw.com

Overview

This short, scenic hike showcases the southern section of Palisades Park, where Spokane Garry (circa 1811–1892), chief of the Spokane tribe, made his home in his later years. Its deep-woods scenery, namesake waterfall, and proximity to town make it a popular choice for families and solo hikers alike. The three crossings of the stream that drains Indian Canyon can make for potentially tricky footing, however, and the trails themselves aren't as well kept as some others in the area. Nevertheless, this hike is accessible in all seasons—and wintertime trekkers may even be rewarded with a stunning view of the waterfall frozen solid.

Route Details

To access the trailhead from your roadside parking spot along Indian Canyon Drive, you go around a gate on the west side of the road, just as it curves north and becomes Indian Canyon Drive. Across the road to the east and south, you can see the fairways of Indian Canyon Golf Course.

A trailhead marker for Trail 121, along with a map board, is just beyond the gate. About 40 yards southwest of the trailhead, you come to a T-intersection—make a sharp right to head north on Trail 121, passing a junction with Trail 107 on your left about 0.1 mile ahead.

Once on the trail proper, the route takes you into a shallow ravine. Old-growth ponderosa pines seclude the area from outside noise, and the trails in this section are both well marked and maintained. About 0.3 mile from the

Palisades Park: Mystic Falls Loop

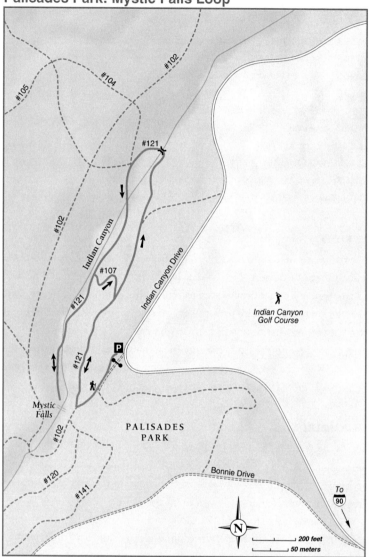

trailhead, you come to the first of three stream crossings, aided by a footbridge made from driftwood. Take care at this crossing and the ones to follow—seniors may wish to bring trekking poles or walking sticks to steady themselves. After the bridge, the trail makes a U-turn left (south), and in a few hundred feet you come to the second creek crossing on a fallen log.

As you progress down into the ravine, brush will be intrusive, and owing to the abundant shallows, mosquitoes will be more prevalent here than at the hike's higher points. Your footing should be more stable in this section, although you should exercise caution in any case.

A large ponderosa pine, on the left less than 0.1 mile past the second creek crossing, displays markers indicating both the trail you're on now, 121, and Trail 107, a connector spur on your left that takes you back to the trailhead (this is the same Trail 107 you passed on the northbound part of the semiloop).

Continue south on Trail 121 another 350 feet to reach the third stream crossing, this one on a log. Then an escarpment splits the trail in two, and around either side of it, the path opens onto Mystic Falls.

The canyon mouth is mostly dry and walkable in summer, with the stream and waterfall barely a trickle; fall and spring hikers, however, will see the falls at their most impressive. The sheer rock rises on all sides, and at the right time of day the sunlight illuminates the entire grotto. The falls themselves make for great photo ops, but also note the two small caves on either side: one up a small cut up the cliff to the right and the other at ground level on the left. Both caves can be explored, but wear good shoes and make multiple points of contact. The cave mouth itself is a great spot to pose for photos, but adventurers should be mindful, as wildlife are known to make it a temporary home on occasion.

After you've had your fill of the falls and the caves, take either side of the trail around the escarpment, and proceed north to start your return trip. When you reach the marked ponderosa pine, now on your right, turn right onto Trail 107 (the connector described earlier) and switchback up the hill. After 200 feet turn right (south) at the T-intersection; then, 0.1 mile ahead, turn left onto the

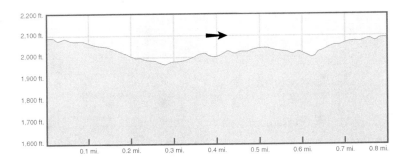

spur leading to the trailhead, and continue on the access path and around the gate to return to your car.

Nearby Attractions

This route conveniently connects with a number of other trails in the southern section of Palisades Park (see the previous hike for an option in the northern section). Other hikes nearby include the popular **Bowl and Pitcher Loop** in Riverside State Park (see next hike) and the Cheney Trailhead to Fish Lake segment of the **Columbia Plateau State Park Trail** (see Hike 1, page 24); you'll find even more options in **People's Park,** near the confluence of Latah Creek and the Spokane River. Golfers can also enjoy a leisurely afternoon on the links at **Indian Canyon Golf Course,** just across Indian Canyon Drive from the trailhead access gate.

Directions

From Monroe Street in downtown Spokane, take I-90 westbound for about 2.4 miles; then take Exit 277 for US 2 West toward Davenport. After about 0.1 mile, get into the far right lane, signed for Garden Springs. Follow the hairpin curve; then, in 0.3 mile, turn left (north) onto South Rustle Road. In 0.1 mile, take another left onto West Sunset Boulevard, heading northwest; then, in another 0.1 mile, turn right (north) onto South Assembly Street. Drive 0.7 mile; then bear left as the road changes to Indian Canyon Drive. In 0.1 mile, watch for the gated access path on the left, marked by boulders on either side of the gate. Park wherever you can find a spot close by along the road, taking care not to block the gate.

STREAMBED ACCESS NEAR THE FALLS

11 Riverside State Park:
Bowl and Pitcher Loop

SCENERY: ★ ★ ★ ★ ★
TRAIL CONDITION: ★ ★ ★ ★ ★
CHILDREN: ★ ★ ★ ★ ★
DIFFICULTY: ★ ★
SOLITUDE: ★ ★

THESE BASALT FORMATIONS LOOK SORT OF LIKE A BOWL AND PITCHER.

GPS TRAILHEAD COORDINATES: N47° 41.751' W117° 29.744'

DISTANCE & CONFIGURATION: 2.1-mile balloon

HIKING TIME: 1 hour

HIGHLIGHTS: Swinging Bridge, rock formations, views of the Spokane River

ELEVATION: 1,642' at lowest point, 1,809' at highest

ACCESS: Daily, 8 a.m.–sunset in winter, 6:30 a.m.–sunset in summer. A Washington State Parks Discover Pass ($10/day, $30/year) is required for parking.

MAPS: USGS *Spokane NW, WA* and *Airway Heights, WA*; maps.spokanecity.org

FACILITIES: Restrooms, picnic tables, picnic pavilion, and paved parking at trailhead; restrooms and water at campground; vault toilets at Centennial Trail–Trail 25 junction; visitor center at park entrance

WHEELCHAIR ACCESS: Only the initial segment including the Swinging Bridge

COMMENTS: Dogs must be leashed; hikers share the trail with cyclists.

CONTACTS: Riverside State Park, 509-465-5064, parks.state.wa.us/573/riverside

Riverside State Park: Bowl and Pitcher Loop

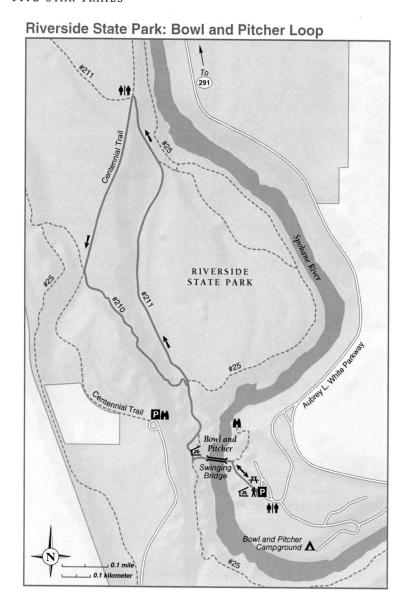

Overview

This trail in Nine Mile Recreation Area, within Riverside State Park, attracts outdoor-fun seekers with stunning views, well-maintained trails, and convenient access to camping. Families and solo hikers alike will find something to enjoy, though this popularity comes at the cost of solitude. This hike is perfect for an early-afternoon excursion with children.

Route Details

The trailhead for this hike can be accessed directly from the western parking loop for Riverside State Park's Bowl and Pitcher Campground. The trail heads straight (west) and then curves left (north) for about 0.1 mile before depositing you at the eastern entrance to the Bowl and Pitcher Swinging Bridge. This picturesque landmark, built in 1933 by the Civilian Conservation Corps, is popular with tourists and travelers. Enjoy close-up views of the Spokane River and the large basalt rock formations that stand sentinel on both sides of the shoreline to the right (north). Take time for photos if you're so inclined. The name *Bowl and Pitcher*, by the way, comes from two local rock formations that resemble a pitcher and a bowl turned sideways.

Exit the bridge on a small set of concrete stairs on the far (west) side; then turn right (north) at the fork. A few yards ahead, a dirt path on your right leads to a picnic shelter–rest area; for now, though, proceed north on Trail 25. Note the brown signposts that are helpfully placed at many trail junctions along the route.

The trail is broad and smooth, so feel free to set your own pace. Climbing enthusiasts will find lots to enjoy here: the basalt rocks are perfect for bouldering, with ample handholds and routes that will appeal to all levels of skill. Use crash pads and other safety equipment as necessary, and as always, be considerate of other visitors.

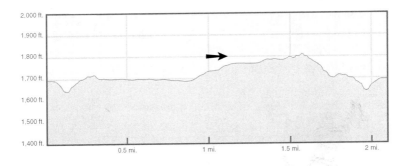

About 0.3 mile from the trailhead, you come to a three-way junction where Trail 25 heads right (east), Trail 210 heads left (west), and Trail 211 continues straight—proceed north on Trail 211. This marks the beginning of the loop portion of the hike.

The trail winds north and east into a patch of dense forest before transitioning to wide, packed-dirt doubletrack. Watch out for cyclists, and pace yourself accordingly—the trail in much of this section climbs steadily. Nevertheless, parents with small children in hiking packs will be a common sight, a testament to this trail's family-friendly appeal. Dogs are also welcome, though their owners must keep them leashed. The frequent warning signs to this effect aren't just for show: wild animals lurk just off the trail, and many a curious canine has come away with a snout full of porcupine quills.

One of the great virtues of this hike lies in the bountiful opportunities for photography. This trail has it all: the Spokane River just to the east, sun-dappled pine forests, towering cliffs, serene woodland meadows, and ample wildlife. With a good digital camera or a decent phone camera, even amateur shutterbugs are sure to come away with pleasing shots.

About 0.8 mile into the hike, bear left at an unmarked junction where a dirt path leads toward the river on the right. Then, about 0.2 mile ahead, make a sharp turn left (south) onto the wide, paved Spokane River Centennial Trail; a restroom building just across the trail marks the turn.

About 0.4 mile from the previous junction, the Centennial Trail sprouts an unpaved offshoot to the left, marked as Trail 210—note the three boulders placed just in front of the signpost. Take this trail and descend a series of gentle switchbacks heading southeast. Morning and afternoon hikers will find the best opportunities for photography in this stretch, as the light through the trees will be strong and the view of the trails below more commanding. Be mindful of your footing, however, as this last leg grows considerably narrower and the drops much steeper.

After about 1.7 miles of hiking, you'll close the loop back at the three-way junction you passed earlier—bear right to head south again on the balloon string, also known as Trail 25. If you need a break, look for the picnic shelter about 0.1 mile ahead, through the trees and just off the dirt path to your left. Take a few moments here to hydrate, catch your breath, or perhaps even wander down to the river's edge and dip your toes in the water. When you're ready, hang a left at the junction back behind the shelter; then descend the stairs and cross back over the Swinging Bridge to the parking area.

Nearby Attractions

Riverside State Park and Nine Mile Recreation Area host numerous other hiking trails. Camping is also available near the trailhead at **Bowl and Pitcher Campground,** which has restrooms as well as showers and RV hookups for those interested in more than a day trip. For even more hiking, check out **Palisades Park** (see Hikes 9 and 10, pages 64 and 68), as well as the **Deep Creek Canyon Loop** (see next hike) and the Cheney Trailhead to Fish Lake segment of the **Columbia Plateau State Park Trail** (see Hike 1, page 24). Or try a relaxing round of disc golf at **People's Park.** Hiking can make you work up an appetite, of course, so swing back through town for a bite to eat at one of the Lilac City's numerous restaurants or food trucks.

Directions

From Spokane, take I-90 westbound to Exit 280A for the Maple Street Bridge. At the end of the ramp, continue straight for one block on West Fourth Avenue; then turn right (north) onto North Walnut Street. In 0.2 mile (two blocks), bear slightly left to continue north on Walnut Street, which soon becomes North Maple Street; then, in about 0.4 mile, cross the Spokane River on the Maple Street Bridge. Continue north on Maple Street for about 1.2 miles; then take a left onto Maxwell Avenue, which curves left (north) and becomes North Pettet Drive after 0.3 mile. Continue west on North Pettet Drive for 0.8 mile; then bear slightly left at the fork to keep heading west; Pettet changes to Downriver Drive. In about 3.5 miles, bear left at the signed turnoff for Riverside State Park; then turn left again, and drive south about 0.2 mile to the parking area for Bowl and Pitcher Campground.

Riverside State Park:
Deep Creek Canyon Loop

SCENERY: ★ ★ ★ ★
TRAIL CONDITION: ★ ★ ★
CHILDREN: ★ ★
DIFFICULTY: ★ ★ ★ ★
SOLITUDE: ★ ★ ★ ★ ★

BRIDGE CROSSING ON THE DEEP CREEK CANYON LOOP

GPS TRAILHEAD COORDINATES: N47° 46.314' W117° 33.125'

DISTANCE & CONFIGURATION: 5.6-mile loop

HIKING TIME: 2 hours

HIGHLIGHTS: Rock formations, views of the Spokane River, access to Spokane River Centennial Trail

ELEVATION: 1,605' at lowest point, 2,200' at highest

ACCESS: Daily, 8 a.m.–sunset in winter, 6:30 a.m.–sunset in summer. A Washington State Parks Discover Pass ($10/day, $30/year) is required for parking.

MAPS: USGS *Nine Mile Falls, WA*; maps.spokanecity.org and at trailhead

FACILITIES: Restrooms, map board, and parking at Carlson Road and Deep Creek Canyon Trailheads; rest areas along route

WHEELCHAIR ACCESS: No

COMMENTS: Dogs must be leashed; hikers share the trail with cyclists. This hike is best attempted by those with strong route-finding skills.

CONTACTS: Riverside State Park, 509-465-5064, parks.state.wa.us/573/riverside

Overview

This trail offers the best views of any hike within Riverside State Park. The catch: inconsistent trail conditions and sparse signage can make it easy to get lost. Whatever navigational aids you have at your disposal—be they maps, compass, or GPS—are highly recommended, as is studying the route before you head out.

Route Details

The gated trailhead is directly across Carlson Road from the parking area. Pass through the gate (or walk around it), and head straight (south) on the paved Spokane River Centennial Trail, which runs close to the Spokane River. Numerous marked rest areas line the route; use the benches as needed, and perhaps snap a photo or two. Local weather conditions often result in low fog over the water, making for a breathtaking early-morning view.

Continuing south on the Centennial Trail, you pass a small picnic area on your right just shy of 0.7 mile from the trailhead; then, just ahead, you cross a trestle bridge over a small inlet. At this point the elevation begins to rise, and hikers can see a few of the region's numerous pillars of volcanic basalt across the river. These stunning rock formations are great for rock-climbing enthusiasts and are a visual highlight for this portion of the trail. About 0.3 mile past the bridge, you leave the Centennial Trail: look for an unmarked dirt path that makes a sharp right, and get on it heading west for 0.3 mile; then keep left as the trail curves slightly to the left (west and south) and passes a scenic overlook on your right.

As you continue south, the trail widens and becomes more well defined, and about 2 miles from the trailhead (or about 0.5 mile from the previous junction), you reach the gated Deep Creek Canyon Trailhead. Pick up the trail at the far end of the parking area, heading straight (south) where the park road curves to the left (east).

The route passes another junction with a trail on your left in about 0.1 mile and then crosses the dry bed of Deep Creek about 0.1 mile after that. Eventually, you come to a marker for a bicycle trail—take a right here, heading southwest. By now the route has opened into a broad grassy clearing, studded by ponderosas. Then, almost 2.5 miles into the hike, you reach the Pine Bluff

Riverside State Park: Deep Creek Canyon Loop

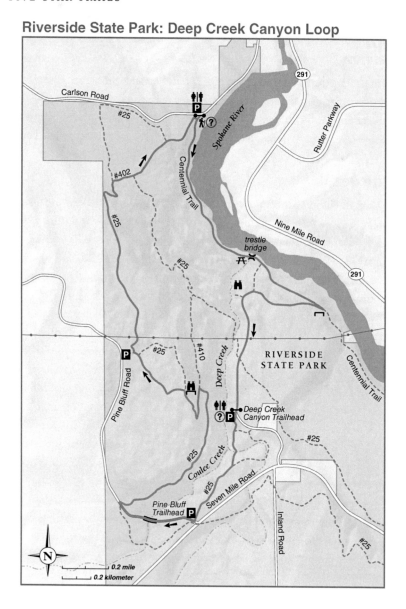

Trailhead, marked by a wooden fence. Continue straight (south) through the parking area; then, with Seven Mile Road to your left (south), turn right (northwest) to walk carefully on the shoulder of Pine Bluff Road.

The trail soon begins to rise, and in about 0.15 mile, the road gives way to a narrow concrete bridge over Coulee Creek. Use care here, as the bridge is rated for vehicle traffic and has no designated pedestrian or cyclist lanes. About 0.1 mile after you cross the bridge, leave the road and turn right onto signed Trail 25, heading northeast.

Note: As you traverse the second half of the loop, it will be extremely important to reorient at regular intervals. The route is signed only sporadically, and the path becomes indistinct in places, so make use of maps, compass, and GPS to stay on course.

Trail 25 generally parallels Coulee Creek as it stretches northeast and gains elevation; Deep Creek and Coulee Creek Canyons and their environs are visible through the trees to your right (south). About 3.35 miles into the hike, the trail straightens, heading due north before curving gradually left (west). The trail is now rocky and rooty, and fallen logs and branches litter the path in places. Step carefully, and stop to rest as needed. At about 3.6 miles, with a steep, rocky drop-off on your right, make a hairpin turn left (south) onto signed Trail 410. Over approximately the next 0.3 mile, the trail makes its greatest gains in elevation.

The trail here is more well defined and free of debris as it climbs a shady ridge, but with a fairly steep drop-off to the left (east), you still need to be careful as you proceed south. At 3.75 total miles, you make another hairpin turn to the right, heading northwest. You now ascend the ridgeline, with another steep drop-off to your right (north) and occasional views through the trees. At about 3.8 miles, the terrain levels and then enters a clearing; a scenic overlook to the

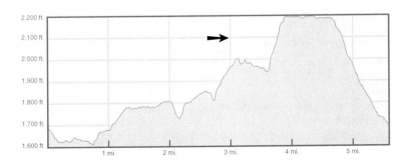

right affords photo-worthy views of the Spokane River to the north. A bench here provides a place to rest.

Past the overlook, the trail is broad, smooth, and flat as it proceeds north-northwest. At 3.9 miles (about 0.5 mile past the overlook), turn left (west) at the junction onto Trail 25 (look for the signpost on the right). From here, the trail remains mostly level as it curves right (north); note that the path itself in this section is poorly defined at times, so pull out your map and compass/GPS as needed. In about 300 feet, just past a signpost on your right, swing right (northeast) to continue on Trail 25.

The trail remains mostly level as it proceeds north, passing under power lines at a little more than 4 total miles. A few yards past the power lines, fallen branches and logs litter (but don't block) the path; then the trail bends slightly left (northwest). The path is once again level, well defined, and easy to follow in this stretch as it carves its way through the pines. Starting at around 4.7 miles, the trail starts to lose elevation as it enters its home stretch.

At about 4.9 miles, you turn sharply right (east); then, about 300 feet farther, just past another signpost on your left for Trail 25, you switchback left (north). Then, about 0.1 mile after that, you reach a signed junction where Trail 25 continues north—turn right (northeast) onto Trail 402. Along this final descent, you pass signed junctions with Trail 25 on your right (at about 5.1 miles) and your left (just shy of 5.4 miles). Finally, after a little more than 5.5 miles of hiking, you make a final swing right, following a narrow dirt trail down a steep embankment to once again meet the paved Centennial Trail; then turn left (north), pass through (or around) the gate, and cross Carlson Road to reach the parking area.

Nearby Attractions

For more hiking opportunities in Riverside State Park, see the previous and following hikes. The park also offers excellent camping, fishing, and summertime recreation. **Nine Mile Falls Dam** is also tantalizingly close, as is **Palisades Park** (see Hikes 9 and 10, pages 64 and 68).

Directions

From Spokane, take I-90 westbound to Exit 280A for the Maple Street Bridge. At the end of the ramp, continue straight for one block on West Fourth Avenue;

then turn right (north) onto North Walnut Street. In 0.2 mile (two blocks), bear slightly left to continue north on Walnut Street, which soon becomes North Maple Street; then, in about 0.4 mile, cross the Spokane River on the Maple Street Bridge. Continue north on Maple Street for about 1.4 miles; then turn left (northwest) onto Northwest Boulevard. In 0.7 mile, turn right (north) onto North Cochran Street. In 0.3 mile, Cochran curves left and becomes North Driscoll Boulevard. In 2.2 miles, turn left across North Assembly Street; then bear left (west) again onto WA 291/West Francis Avenue/West Nine Mile Road. In 6.1 miles, turn left onto Charles Road and continue across the Spokane River; then take the first left across the bridge onto Carlson Road, heading south. The trailhead parking area is about 0.3 mile ahead on the right.

WOODLAND CLEARING ON THE DEEP CREEK CANYON LOOP

13 # Riverside State Park:
Trail 25 to Spokane River Centennial Trail

SCENERY: ★ ★ ★
TRAIL CONDITION: ★ ★ ★ ★ ★
CHILDREN: ★ ★ ★ ★ ★
DIFFICULTY: ★
SOLITUDE: ★

ALONG THE SPOKANE RIVER IN RIVERSIDE STATE PARK   photographed by Elizabeth Marlin

GPS TRAILHEAD COORDINATES: N47° 45.252' W117° 32.926'

DISTANCE & CONFIGURATION: 3.8-mile out-and-back

HIKING TIME: 1.5 hours

HIGHLIGHTS: Views of Deep Creek and Spokane River, well-groomed trails, disability access, scenic overlooks, camping nearby

ELEVATION: 1,659' at lowest point, 1,807' at highest

ACCESS: Daily, 8 a.m.–sunset in winter, 6:30 a.m.–sunset in summer. A Washington State Parks Discover Pass ($10/day, $30/year) is required for parking.

MAPS: USGS *Nine Mile Falls, WA;* maps.spokanecity.org and at trailhead

FACILITIES: Restrooms, map board, and parking at both trailheads; picnic table and scenic overlook at McLellan Trailhead

WHEELCHAIR ACCESS: Yes

COMMENTS: Dogs must be leashed; hikers share the trail with cyclists

CONTACTS: Riverside State Park, 509-465-5064, parks.state.wa.us/573/riverside

Overview

This hike, which shares part of its route with the Deep Creek Canyon Loop (see previous hike), takes in a 2-mile out-and-back section of the Spokane River Centennial Trail, a 38-mile paved route that stretches east from Post Falls, Idaho, to Nine Mile Falls, Washington. The trail's broad, smooth, level surfaces make it very popular with hikers, cyclists, and families, and it passes through several state and county parks—Riverside State Park among them—thus providing manageable segments for the casual hiker. Note that the trail sees heavy pedestrian traffic, and on this hike in particular you won't find much in the way of solitude.

Route Details

Begin at the Deep Creek Canyon Trailhead. Park in the dirt lot near the gate, and head straight (north) on Trail 25. The trail here is hard-packed dirt, suitable for both hikers and cyclists, as well as for families with children. Depending on the season, the only gear you need is a pair of comfortable shoes and perhaps a jacket.

A few considerations: This trail is popular and heavily trafficked all along its length, in part because it remains snow-free and accessible for large portions of the year. Altitude differences range no more than 150 feet and should be gentle enough for most visitors with minimal exertion. Though the trail gets especially busy on weekends and during holidays, morning hikers will find that

Riverside State Park:
Trail 25 to Spokane River Centennial Trail

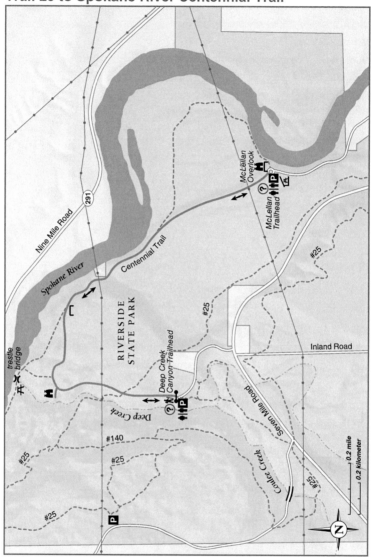

they have the path almost entirely to themselves. Feel free to listen to music, jog, or even push a toddler in a stroller, but note that cyclists also share the trail, so be conscientious of others. As with many other trails on this list, dogs are also welcome, though they must remain leashed at all times.

About 0.2 mile ahead, keep straight at a signed junction where Trail 25 heads left. Be mindful, as the signage doesn't indicate a trail and this turn can be easily missed. About 0.1 mile past the intersection, you pass under power lines, and to your left (west) views open into Deep Creek Canyon, with gorgeous vistas of stark cliffs overhead as well as pine forest and the creek itself below.

Note that at several points, there are small turnouts for scenic overlooks—one, for example, is on your left (west) at almost 0.5 mile from the Deep Creek Canyon Trailhead. Wander to these as the impulse arises; then return to the main trail and continue north. Note that not all turnoffs are marked, so it probably wouldn't hurt to have your phone, GPS, or a supplemental map and compass handy in addition to the map in this book.

About 0.1 past the overlook noted previously, the trail passes a junction with a spur to your left and begins to curve gently to the right (east), and the trail begins to rise. A little more than 0.3 mile farther, you merge with the paved Centennial Trail proper, heading right (southeast) and downhill. Just past the fork, a bench on your right provides a place to rest a bit. Overlooks to your left (east) afford views of the Spokane River.

As the trail descends and traverses closer to the river, the views get even better. Photo ops abound, and anywhere in this stretch would make a great place for a picnic. However, it's not a good choice for a summer swim: the slopes leading down to the river are steep, and there are no beaches to speak of. Nine Mile Falls Recreation Area, a few miles north of here, has no shortage of better opportunities, all within easy driving distance.

After 1.9 total miles of hiking, you arrive at the McLellan Trailhead, which has additional parking, restrooms, a map kiosk, a shaded picnic table,

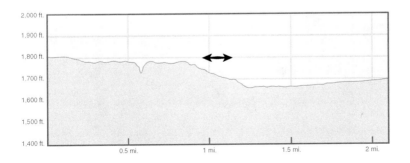

and a scenic overlook with a bench. Take some time here to rest up, check the map, snap some photos, or enjoy a snack before returning the way you came.

Nearby Attractions

For additional hiking opportunities in Riverside State Park, see the previous two hikes. For even more outdoor fun, check out **Palisades Park** (see Hikes 9 and 10, pages 64 and 68) and **People's Park.** Located in the northwest section of Riverside State Park, **Nine Mile Recreation Area** offers camping, along with swimming and boating on Nine Mile Reservoir in the summer.

Directions

From Spokane, take I-90 westbound to Exit 280A for the Maple Street Bridge. At the end of the ramp, continue straight for one block on West Fourth Avenue; then turn right (north) onto North Walnut Street. In 0.2 mile (two blocks), bear slightly left to continue north on Walnut Street, which soon becomes North Maple Street; then, in about 0.4 mile, cross the Spokane River on the Maple Street Bridge. Continue north on Maple Street for about 1.4 miles; then turn left (northwest) onto Northwest Boulevard. In 0.7 mile, turn right (north) onto North Cochran Street. In 0.3 mile, Cochran curves left and becomes North Driscoll Boulevard. In 2.2 miles, turn left across North Assembly Street; then bear left (west) again onto WA 291/West Francis Avenue/West Nine Mile Road. In 2.1 miles, turn left (northwest) onto North Seven Mile Road; then, in 0.6 mile, cross the Spokane River and continue west onto West Seven Mile Road. In 1.5 miles, turn right (north) onto North State Park Drive, and follow it about 0.4 mile to the parking area for the Deep Creek Canyon Trailhead.

RAPIDS OVERLOOK ALONG THE CENTENNIAL TRAIL   photographed by Elizabeth Marlin

City Center

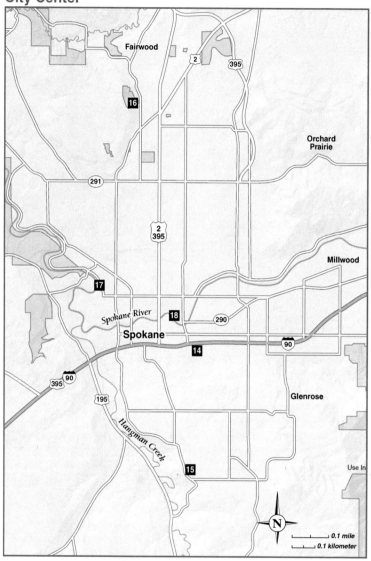

Fairwood

Orchard Prairie

Millwood

291

2 395

17

Spokane River 18 290

Spokane

14

395 90

195

Glenrose

15

Use In

N

0.1 mile
0.1 kilometer

City Center

THE SPOKANE RIVER AS SEEN FROM THE WEST CENTRAL BLUFF (SEE HIKE 17, PAGE 107)

SCENERY: ★ ★ ★ ★
TRAIL CONDITION: ★ ★ ★ ★ ★
CHILDREN: ★ ★ ★ ★ ★
DIFFICULTY: ★
SOLITUDE: ★ ★

BASAL ESCARPMENTS ALONG THE BEN BURR TRAIL

GPS TRAILHEAD COORDINATES: N47° 39.167' W117° 23.310'

DISTANCE & CONFIGURATION: 2.3-mile out-and-back

HIKING TIME: 0.25 hours

HIGHLIGHTS: Impeccable trail conditions, proximity to historic Perry District, views of Beacon Hill

ELEVATION: 1,889' at lowest point, 2,015' at highest

ACCESS: Daily, 6 a.m.–10 p.m.; no fees or permits

MAPS: USGS *Spokane NW, WA*; maps.spokanecity.org and at trailhead

FACILITIES: Picnic areas, map board, trash can, and paved parking at trailhead

WHEELCHAIR ACCESS: Yes

COMMENTS: This trail has an optional unpaved segment that runs from just north of East 11th Avenue to Underhill Park; dogs must be leashed; hikers share the trail with cyclists

CONTACTS: Spokane City Parks and Recreation, 509-625-6200, my.spokanecity.org/parksrec

Overview

Just 10 minutes from downtown and situated along the boundary between Spokane's Perry and East Central Districts, Ben Burr is a beloved local trail, accessible from Liberty Park or, alternatively, from the trailhead addition at nearby Underhill Park. Exceptionally popular with hikers and cyclists, this paved out-and-back trail with gentle grades and dense foliage is also great for families, as well as older and disabled hikers.

Route Details

Begin this hike at Liberty Park. Take a moment here to survey your surroundings: the trailhead is clearly visible just south of the parking area, though the park's vast public green spaces provide ample space to linger a moment and get your bearings. Consider bringing a picnic lunch for either before or after the hike; the nearby pavilion off to your left also provides an ideal resting spot, even on rainy days. For now, however, follow the sidewalk pathway to the trailhead. Based on need and personal preference, either take the disability access to the left or proceed straight up the hill.

After you crest the small hill at the trail's entrance, you'll first notice the high cliff walls on either side of the path. The exposed rock is the same basalt common to much of this area. These formations developed hundreds of thousands of years in the past, when a combination of volcanic activity and massive glacial-period floods put down a layer of rapidly cooled igneous material from inside the earth's mantle. These violent natural upheavals give the area's soils their trademark fertility, shaping the region's influence as a major timber and agricultural producer. Take a moment to marvel at the millennia of history bound up in these rocks, and the titanic feats of human engineering necessary to carve a path through them. Continue up the trail when ready.

The Ben Burr Trail was renovated in 2016, upgrading to pavement from a combination of soil and gravel. This makes Ben Burr a prime trail for cyclists, as well as for hikers using wheelchairs or other assistive mobility devices. A little more than 0.25 from the trailhead, the path leaves the park and proceeds nearly ramrod straight, heading southeast along a gentle rise. From here, hikers should have a clear view of the sleepy residential neighborhoods that make up East

Ben Burr Trail

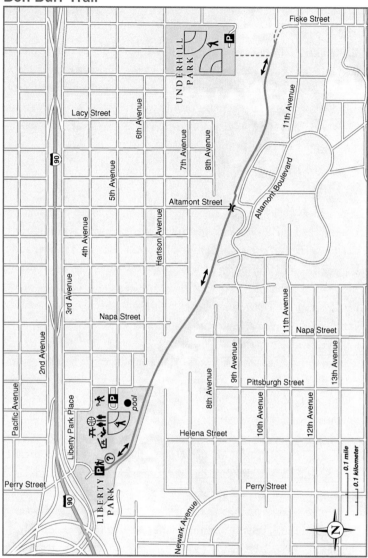

Central and, more distantly, views of the East Sprague commercial district and its signature high-rise grain elevator. Beyond these, on clear days, you can even make out Beacon Hill, which also features in the loop trail of the same name (see Hike 20, page 124, for more information).

This hike is distinguished not just by its straightforward nature and ease of access but also by the diversity of its flora. Where much of the region is dominated by a mixture of ponderosa and lodgepole pine, Ben Burr is situated along the windward boundary of the Spokane Valley. This fact, combined with the trail's elevation, places it in an ideal spot to receive ample rainfall, most commonly in the winter and spring, which nurtures all manner of deciduous and flowering growth along the length of the route. Astute hikers will note large stands of maple, oak, ash, and even beech, which are otherwise uncommon in the relatively dry climes of the Inland Northwest. The dense broadleaf canopies overhead make for great photography and also provide welcome shade during the oppressive summer heat.

As you progress, the trail continues to rise, providing a clear view of the entire Spokane Valley. At a little more than 0.7 mile from the trailhead, you come to a small, fenced-in trestle bridge over South Altamont Street—cross it and continue on. Shortly after the bridge, the trail will begin to curve gently to the right—follow it upward until the yellow traffic barriers become visible. Those with an enterprising spirit can continue to the left, following the optional unpaved addition north about 0.1 mile to Underhill Park. Beyond this, the main portion of the trail terminates at a vehicle barricade, just north of East 11th Avenue and a quiet residential area, at 1.15 miles. Return the way you came.

Nearby Attractions

This hike lies right in the heart of metro Spokane and is thus close to many of the things that make the Lilac City a great place to live. Just around the

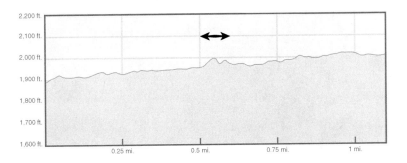

corner lies Spokane's historic **Perry District,** which offers a wealth of excellent dining options and in summer plays host to a variety of farmers' markets and street fairs. Additionally, the commercial stretch of **East Sprague** has undergone a striking renovation in recent years, transforming it from a symbol of urban decay to a thriving area of quaint shops and pubs.

Directions

From South Division Street in downtown Spokane, head east on Third Avenue. In 0.5 mile, the road forks—continue straight on Third Avenue where South Sprague Way heads left (north). In 0.2 mile, just after you cross Arthur Street, the road curves right (south) and passes under the I-90/US-290 junction. In another 0.3 mile, turn right onto Liberty Park Place; then make another quick right into the trailhead parking area.

YOU CROSS THIS TRESTLE BRIDGE ABOUT 0.7 MILE FROM THE TRAILHEAD.

15 Hangman Park Loop

SCENERY: ★ ★ ★ ★ ★
TRAIL CONDITION: ★ ★ ★
CHILDREN: ★ ★ ★ ★
DIFFICULTY: ★ ★ ★
SOLITUDE: ★ ★ ★ ★

HEADING DOWN INTO THE CANYON ON HANGMAN PARK LOOP

GPS TRAILHEAD COORDINATES: N47° 36.142' W117° 23.650'

DISTANCE & CONFIGURATION: 3.75-mile loop

HIKING TIME: 1.75 hours

HIGHLIGHTS: Views of Latah Creek Gorge; plenty of old-growth forest cover; large, open wilderness spaces

ELEVATION: 1,851' at lowest point, 2,379' at highest

ACCESS: Daily, 6 a.m.–10 p.m.; no fees or permits

MAPS: USGS *Spokane SW, WA;* maps.spokanecity.org

FACILITIES: Gravel parking lot at trailhead

WHEELCHAIR ACCESS: No

COMMENTS: Dogs must be leashed. Because this hike is entirely unmarked and shares space with an elaborate network of bicycle trails, it can be easy to lose your bearings, particularly in the upper reaches. To limit confusion, stick to the route as described here—stay on freshly graded trails only, and avoid bike tracks as well as any switchback-intensive offshoots.

CONTACTS: Spokane City Parks and Recreation, 509-625-6200, my.spokanecity.org/parksrec

Hangman Park Loop

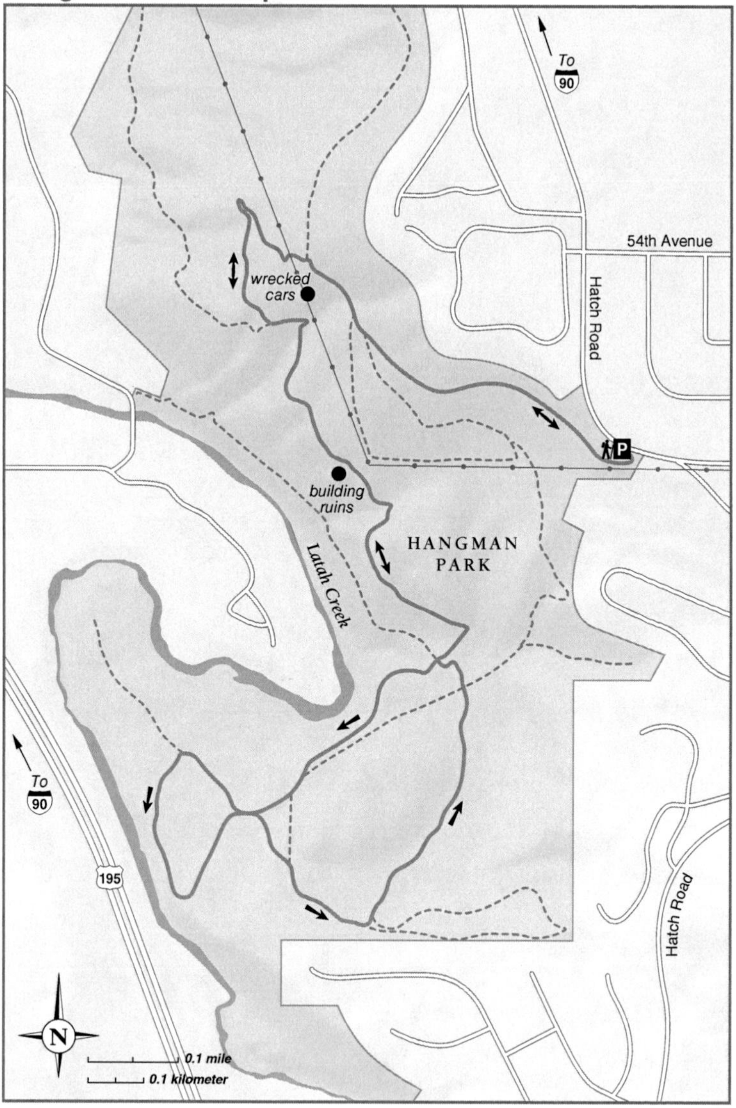

Map labels: To 90; 54th Avenue; Hatch Road; wrecked cars; building ruins; Latah Creek; HANGMAN PARK; P; To 90; 195; Hatch Road; N; 0.1 mile; 0.1 kilometer

Overview

Set against the forested cliffs of the Latah Creek Gorge, this hike is unique in being directly accessible from Spokane's lower South Hill, making it a prime pick for urban hikers looking for something close to home. This unpaved, lightly trafficked route is popular with both hikers and cyclists, boasting breathtaking views and a degree of solitude unmatched anywhere within the city limits.

Route Details

Begin from the gravel parking area on Hatch Road. The trailhead is down a small slope to the left, with views facing west. Note that there are no map boards, trash cans, or restrooms here—all signage clearly states a pack-in/pack-out policy regarding trash and waste (and that includes picking up after pets).

The initial leg of this trail is fairly straightforward: follow the trail down the cliff as it curves slightly right and to the north, passing under power lines at just shy of 0.5 mile. Stay on the clearly marked footpath—offshoots to your left and right are intended for cyclists. The chief exception to this rule comes about 0.6 mile into the hike, when the trail hooks back and to the left nearly 180°. Then you continue south as the forest cover grows more dense. You should be proceeding at this point down a steep, winding draw.

At about 0.7 mile, you come to the first major landmark for this hike: a pair of wrecked automobiles off to your left (east), several decades old by the look of things. These wrecks have become something of a local fixture, given the number of graffiti etchings, bumper stickers, and even bullet holes left behind by visitors, but more importantly they serve as a visual cue to the correct route for hikers. The story of these two cars, their former owners, and how they came to rest here has been lost to local history, but nevertheless they provide a striking memento mori, and a caution to motorists.

Immediately past the second, lower wreck, turn left where the trail is partially obscured by foliage (to the right is a bike trail that will get you off-course).

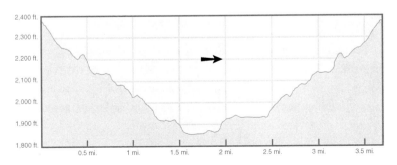

CANYON SECLUSION ABOUNDS ON THIS HIKE.

From here, the trail continues downhill, heading east then south. Hikers should have a clear view of suburban houses below them, along with a view of Latah (also known as Hangman) Creek. Feel free to enjoy the sounds of the rushing water as you descend, and perhaps stop to take in some of the local flora and fauna. Wildflowers are a common sight along this trail in springtime, with wild daisy, currant, snowdrop, and hyacinth all making appearances.

About 0.3 mile past the wrecked cars, you reach what appears to be a ruined building foundation on your right, perched on the edge of a cliff overlooking the creek. Those of an inquiring nature will be rewarded by a small diversion here, as this site has been co-opted by an enterprising graffiti artist, who signs his or her work under the moniker of SMUG. Take a few photos of the detailed murals for posterity, then head down the trail.

At about 1 mile into the hike, the trail swings abruptly left (southwest). Not long afterward, you'll arrive at a fork in the road—continue straight along the rightmost fork.

By this time, hikers will find themselves at the bottom of the gorge, close to the creek and nearly to the halfway point of this hike. The route from here consists of a 1.2-mile butterfly loop, so named for reasons that will shortly become apparent. Continue down the trail, making note of the vast open meadows and dense stands of ponderosa and lodgepole pine. This area is a prime spot for photography, though again you should be wary of wandering too far off the trail. The underbrush here is prone to ticks (see page 18). Make note of the hairpin turn on the upper edge of the butterfly—keep right to stay on the trail. Eventually, you come to a pair of doubletracks, which appear to merge and then separate in a distinct X shape. This bottleneck forms the center of the butterfly—keep to the rightmost path and continue counterclockwise along the loop.

After rounding back through the second crossover of the X, keep right (southeast). At 2.1 miles turn left (northeast) at a junction, and continue 0.3 mile to the four-way fork at the outset of the loop; then turn right (northeast) and return the way you came. Follow the aforementioned landmarks to keep your bearings, and eventually you'll find yourself back at the trailhead.

Nearby Attractions

This trail's location on the edge of Spokane's South Hill neighborhood makes it an appealing hike for those who live in town—it also provides access to some of the Lilac City's greatest attractions. Stop at nearby **Manito Park** to feed some ducks, visit the famed Lilac and Rose Gardens, or just let your kids loose on the playground. If you're hungry, you have a wide variety of dining options—check out **Luna** (lunaspokane.com) for upscale dishes, or try **Poole's Public House–South** (poolespublichouse.com), **Manito Tap House** (manitotaphouse.com), or **RepublicPi** (republicpi.com) for casual fare such as vegetarian burgers and artisanal pizza. If you're looking for something a little more cosmopolitan, **Gordy's Sichuan Cafe** (gordysspokane.com) regularly tops local best-of lists for Asian food.

Directions

From I-90 westbound, take Exit 280A for Maple Street/Walnut Street. At the end of the ramp, go straight (west) for two blocks on West Fourth Avenue; then turn left (south) onto South Maple Street, and use the right two lanes to proceed up the hill. In about 0.5 mile, Maple Street curves left and then right and merges with South Cedar Street—follow the road south for 0.7 mile, and just past West 21st Avenue, Cedar becomes South High Drive Parkway. After roughly 1.4 miles, High Drive Parkway transitions back to West High Drive. In another 1.1 miles, turn right (south) onto South Scott Street, which becomes South Hatch Road. After about 1 mile, the Hatch Drive parking area will be on your right.

Holmberg Community Park and Conservation Area Loop

SCENERY: ★ ★ ★ ★ ★
TRAIL CONDITION: ★ ★
CHILDREN: ★ ★ ★
DIFFICULTY: ★ ★ ★
SOLITUDE: ★ ★ ★ ★

AFTER A SHADELESS TREK, THE PATH ENTERS THE COOL SHADOWS OF THE FOREST.

GPS TRAILHEAD COORDINATES: N47° 44.684' W117° 25.452'

DISTANCE & CONFIGURATION: 1.4-mile loop

HIKING TIME: 0.75 hours

HIGHLIGHTS: Secluded hiking close to town, dense forest growth, great views of the entire Spokane Valley

ELEVATION: 1,961' at lowest point, 2,247' at highest

ACCESS: Daily, sunrise–sunset; no fees or permits

MAPS: USGS *Spokane NW, WA;* maps.spokanecity.org

FACILITIES: Restrooms, trash cans, and paved parking at trailhead

WHEELCHAIR ACCESS: No

COMMENTS: Dogs must be leashed

CONTACTS: Spokane County Parks, Recreation & Golf, 509-477-4730, spokanecounty.org/facilities/facility/details/holmberg-community-park-37

Overview

Just south of the Whitworth University campus, this brisk hike showcases stunning prairie and forest views. At less than 2 miles, it's a great choice for families with older kids, though older hikers may wish to bring trekking poles, and the trail condition makes it a poor choice for disabled visitors.

Route Details

Begin this hike from the paved lot at Holmberg Community Park. The trailhead itself is just west of the lot, around the other side of the tennis courts. Proceed to the right and keep straight (west)—there will be a slight rise, at which point the route ahead becomes clear. Be sure to snap a few photos, as this spot opens onto a large, grassy meadow framed by pine-blanketed hills.

Follow the trail as it curves slightly to the right (north). There will be numerous potential turnoffs along this route, but stick to the widest path—though this isn't the best-maintained trail in this guide, it should still be clear enough. About 0.1 mile from the start, the terrain begins to rise, and the current path intersects the closing section of the loop. For this hike, keep slightly to the right and then follow the bend around to the left, heading northwest.

At this point, the terrain transitions from grassland to ponderosa and lodgepole pine—standard for the dry Eastern Washington landscape. Like the rest of the region in which it is situated, this hike lies within an ecotone, or transitional biome, between the Palouse, the Channeled Scablands, and the Selkirk

103

Holmberg Community Park and Conservation Area Loop

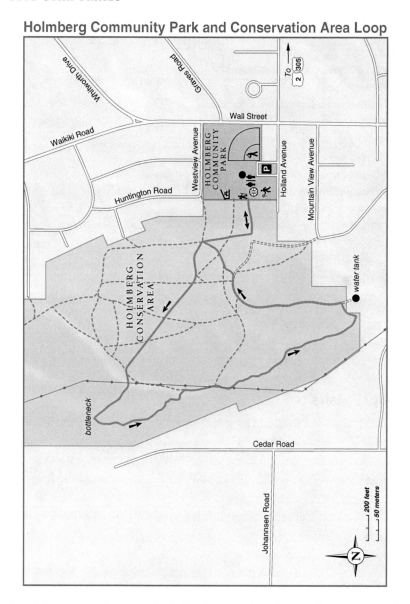

boreal forest. As such, a great deal of biodiversity exists here, making it an appealing spot for educational groups, as well as hikers with an interest in local ecology.

The next 0.2 mile continues on a steady, steep incline, with a grade averaging about 8% and sandy soil that gives way quickly underfoot. Reasonably fit individuals should be fine, though older and disabled hikers would do well to bring trekking poles. Hydration is also key, as this area is known for hot, arid summers, made worse by the heat-retaining properties of the local evergreen trunks. The combination of factors may evoke the feeling of a sauna, with searing hot air and a faint whiff of pine. A reminder: Burn bans are strictly enforced throughout the region.

As the trail continues to rise, you come to what appears to be a slight bottleneck in the trail at about 0.4 mile, with two sections bisecting in an hourglass shape. Many local guides show this as the beginning of an additional loop or balloon, but these guides are in fact out-of-date. Recent home development has swallowed up the left fork, while the right fork juts off to the northwest, following a clear-cut made to accommodate power lines. The trail along this right fork has been allowed to go fallow and thus no longer links back to the main route, so take the hairpin back and to the left (south).

The trail is now at its highest elevation (2,247') and firmly within the leeward side of the hills. This natural wind buffer, coupled with the dense tree cover, leads to cooler, more humid microclimates, providing a welcome respite from the heat. You may also notice yet another transition, as the forest shifts from ponderosa pine to a mixture of spruce and larch. Moss is a common sight, growing both on the ground and on tree trunks, and the dead scrub of the woodland floor gives way to a vibrant, fern-and-flower-rich understory. Take care through here—while the dense underbrush may cultivate an exotic, fairy-woodland vibe, it's also prime territory for spiders and ticks. See page 18 for information on tick prevention, and be sure to check your body and clothing after you've finished hiking.

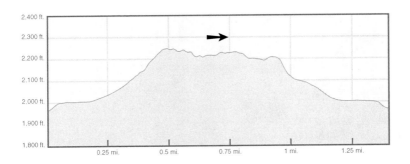

Just shy of 1 mile into the hike, you reach the turnaround point of the loop, heading left (northeast) and passing a water tank to your right. The trail transitions to a series of gentle switchbacks, descending gradually. There are few turnoffs here, so don't worry about getting lost before exiting the woods. Eventually, you reach the treeline, and you should recognize the original meadow from the outset of the hike. Follow the trail as it winds east; then follow the curve to the right to rejoin the original path. Follow this south for a hundred yards or so, and the parking area will once again come into view.

Directions

From Spokane, take I-90 westbound to Exit 280A for Maple Street/Walnut Street. At the end of the ramp, continue straight for one block on West Fourth Avenue; then turn right (north) onto North Walnut Street. In 0.2 mile (two blocks), bear slightly left to continue north on Walnut Street, which soon becomes North Maple Street; then, in about 0.4 mile, cross the Spokane River on the Maple Street Bridge. Continue north on Maple Street for 4.2 miles; the road begins to curve slightly right, becoming North Country Homes Boulevard. In 1.3 miles, turn left (north) onto North Wall Street. After roughly 0.6 mile, turn left onto West Holland Avenue. The trailhead parking area in Holmberg Community Park will be on your right.

THIS TRAIL AFFORDS SWEEPING VIEWS OF THE SPOKANE VALLEY.

17 Spokane River Centennial Trail: West Central to Spokane Falls

SCENERY: ★ ★ ★ ★ ★
TRAIL CONDITION: ★ ★ ★ ★ ★
CHILDREN: ★
DIFFICULTY: ★
SOLITUDE: ★ ★

THE SPOKANE RIVER AS SEEN FROM THE WEST CENTRAL BLUFF OVERLOOK

GPS TRAILHEAD COORDINATES: N47° 40.537' W117° 26.721'

DISTANCE & CONFIGURATION: 6.2-mile out-and-back

HIKING TIME: 2 hours

HIGHLIGHTS: Proximity to downtown; views of Doomsday Hill, Latah Creek, Spokane River, and Spokane Falls

ELEVATION: 1,831' at lowest point, 1,893' at highest

ACCESS: Daily, 6:30 a.m.–sunset (best accessed October–May during daylight hours); no fees or permits

MAPS: USGS *Spokane NW, WA*; maps.spokanecity.org

FACILITIES: Picnic area and parking at trailhead; numerous benches and scenic overlooks along the route

WHEELCHAIR ACCESS: Yes

COMMENTS: The trail sees heavy use by cyclists and runners, so be mindful of your surroundings, and observe proper etiquette. Dogs must be leashed.

CONTACTS: Spokane City Parks and Recreation, 509-625-6200, my.spokanecity.org/parksrec; Friends of the Centennial Trail, 509-624-7188, spokanecentennialtrail.org

Spokane River Centennial Trail: West Central to Spokane Falls

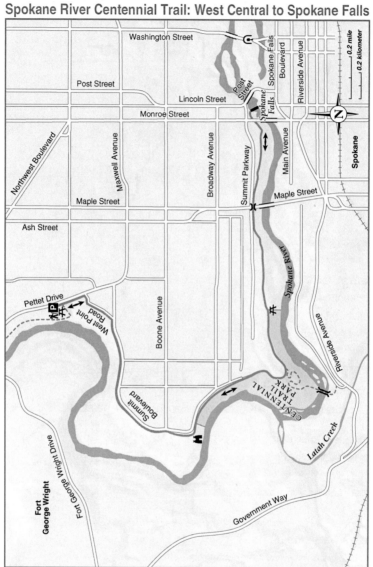

Overview

This hike takes in a small section of the 38-mile-long Spokane River Centennial Trail, which stretches from Nine Mile Falls northwest of Spokane all the way to Post Falls, Idaho. The segment described here extends down through

Kendall Yards before ending at the Monroe Street Bridge and Spokane Falls. This delightful paved trail is great for hikers, cyclists, those with disabilities, and families with small children.

Route Details

Begin from the parking area on North Pettet Drive. To the north, you have a view of Doomsday Hill, a notorious feature of the popular annual Lilac Bloomsday Run. To the west, far below, is the Spokane River. Head south along the side of the road, remaining mindful of both car and bike traffic. After about a block, turn right onto North West Point Road. Note that the trail here becomes separated from the roadway by a curb. Where West Point Drive meets Summit Boulevard, at about 0.3 mile, keep right on Summit.

This initial portion of the hike takes you along the edge of Spokane's historic West Central neighborhood. The first of Spokane's streetcar suburbs, West Central dates back to the turn of the 20th century, when light rail opened up the residential areas just north of the river from downtown. Though the streetcars have long since been decommissioned, many of the rails are still visible, peeking out through the pavement and serving as a testament to the city's industrial history. Make note of the architecture throughout this portion of the hike—West Central is home to some of the oldest single-family homes in Spokane, many of them Craftsman and Victorian-style structures. Enjoy the placid streets and scenic views afforded here, but as a courtesy please restrict photography to the west-facing vistas along the bluff.

At roughly 1 mile into the hike, the trail diverges from Summit Boulevard and becomes a dedicated paved trail, which you'll follow around to the right. At this point, the route begins to descend, leading visitors along the edge of a grassy bluff, with commanding views of the Spokane River and Vinegar Flats on the other side of the gorge. Keep heading south, and before long the homes to your left disappear from view and you skirt the southern edges of West Central. Note historic Fort George Wright across the river—named for a local U.S. Army colonel from the 19th century, the fort's cemetery serves as a final resting place for area veterans dating back to the Spanish-American War. Such reverence for local history, however, is not without its own dark legacies. Just to the left of the fort and cemetery, looking southwest, is Latah Creek tributary, known to

SPOKANE RIVER RAPIDS, WEST CENTRAL

local tribes as Hangman Creek, after a massacre of indigenous peoples there led by Col. Wright.

As the trail winds south, you come to a scenic overlook marked by a retaining wall and several informational placards. Take a few moments to read up on the region's history, and make note of Centennial Trail Park down below. When you're ready, continue on the trail, which now heads east at about 1.8 miles.

You'll now begin to notice an increase in human traffic, due in large part to the trail's proximity to downtown, the skyline of which is visible up ahead. At 2.6 miles, the trail crosses the Maple Street Bridge and continues east. Then, at a little more than 3 miles, you pass under the Monroe Street Bridge before reaching this hike's turnaround point: the mighty Spokane Falls. Built by famed architect Kirtland Cutter, the bridge has stood for more than a century as one of Spokane's great visual icons. A scenic overlook just past the bridge yields stellar views of the falls, which once sustained generations of tribal fishermen and which now provide hydroelectric power to the entire Spokane area and beyond.

When ready, return the way you came or continue across the river into downtown on the Post Street Bridge, just north and east of the falls.

Nearby Attractions

This trail represents a pinnacle of urban hiking, taking you through historic parks and residential neighborhoods, before ending right in the heart of downtown Spokane. It's also noteworthy for its proximity to **Kendall Yards,** comprising a recent spate of developments intended to reclaim abandoned areas of the city. What just a decade past was little more than a series of vacant lots now boasts a wide range of shops and restaurants. With a host of options to entertain both visitors and locals, along with enough seclusion to afford a moment's peace, the Centennial Trail really does provide the best of both worlds.

Directions

From Spokane, take I-90 westbound to Exit 280A for Maple Street/Walnut Street. At the end of the ramp, continue straight for one block on West Fourth Avenue; then turn right (north) onto North Walnut Street. In 0.2 mile (two blocks), bear slightly left to continue north on Walnut Street, which soon becomes North Maple Street; then, in about 0.4 mile, cross the Spokane River on the Maple Street Bridge. Continue across the bridge onto North Maple; then, in 0.6 mile, turn left onto West Maxwell Avenue. Follow the bend right (north) past A. M. Cannon Park on your right, as Maxwell turns into North Pettet Drive. After 0.3 mile, the parking area will be on your left.

18 Spokane River Walk via Centennial Trail and King Cole Way

SCENERY: ★ ★ ★ ★ ★
TRAIL CONDITION: ★ ★ ★ ★ ★
CHILDREN: ★ ★
DIFFICULTY: ★
SOLITUDE: ★

THIS SECTION OF THE CENTENNIAL TRAIL LIES BETWEEN WASHINGTON STATE UNIVERSITY SPOKANE'S RIVERPOINT CAMPUS AND THE SPOKANE CONVENTION CENTER.

GPS TRAILHEAD COORDINATES: N47° 39.830' W117° 24.143'

DISTANCE & CONFIGURATION: 1.9-mile loop

HIKING TIME: 30 minutes

HIGHLIGHTS: Proximity to downtown; views of the Upper Falls; numerous scenic overlooks and art installations along the route

ELEVATION: 1,853' at lowest point, 1,893' at highest

ACCESS: Daily, 6:30 a.m.–sunset. Parking on the Gonzaga University campus, where this hike begins, requires a visitor pass on weekdays during the academic year (call 509-313-4147 or visit gonzaga.edu /about/our-campus-location/parking for more information).

MAPS: USGS Spokane NW, WA; maps.spokanecity.org

FACILITIES: Benches and rest stops along entirety of route; no restrooms except in retail establishments and campus buildings en route

WHEELCHAIR ACCESS: Yes

COMMENTS: Dogs must be leashed

CONTACTS: Spokane City Parks and Recreation, 509-625-6200, my.spokanecity.org/parksrec; Friends of the Centennial Trail, 509-624-7188, spokanecentennialtrail.org

Overview

Located in the heart of downtown Spokane, this hike includes portions of the 38-mile-long Centennial Trail and offers ready access to Gonzaga University, the Spokane Convention Center, and Riverfront Park. It's popular with joggers, families with children, and anyone who works in the city and just wants to get a little fresh air. The paved trail is perfect for hikers of all skill levels, offering abundant green space, art installations, educational displays, and scenic views of the Spokane River. If you seek an urban adventure close to home, look no further.

Route Details

Begin this hike from the parking area just north of the Gonzaga University School of Law. Follow the paved trail west between the parking lot and the law-school building, and cross the bridge over the Spokane River. At the end of the bridge, turn right and continue following the water. The trail is bordered on the left by condominium buildings and abundant flower gardens. A few hundred feet past the bridge, you come to another fork—keep right to stay on the Centennial Trail.

The trail follows a bend, after which point you'll want to keep right, in the direction of Washington State University Spokane's Riverpoint campus. Make note of your location on the accompanying map board, along with any

Spokane River Walk via Centennial Trail and King Cole Way

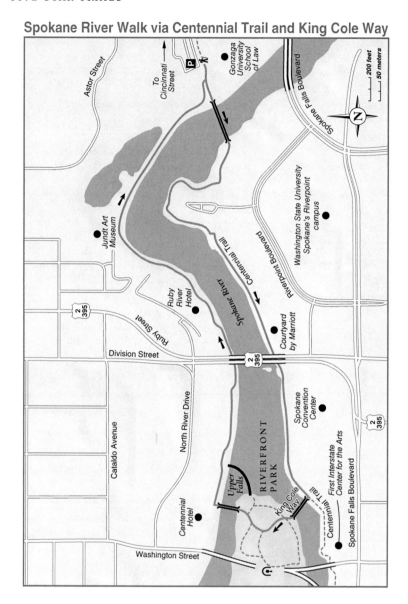

landmarks of interest along the way. This trail is home to a number of stunning art displays, making it a cultural as well as an outdoor experience.

Past the main Riverpoint building, you pass a Courtyard by Marriott hotel on the left at about 0.6 mile—continue west. After passing under the Division

Street Bridge, the trail becomes greener and more enclosed. Make note here of the guardrail to the right: far from being a dilapidated old fence, as it first appears, this actually marks the beginning of a massive art installation, titled *Pathways,* which extends nearly 0.3 mile and traces the history of Spokane through a series of metalwork sculptures integrated into the fence.

The fence display continues; then, at about 0.75 mile, you pass the Spokane Convention Center and the First Interstate Center for the Arts, both on your left. These venues host a wide variety of conventions, conferences, plays, and concerts every year. Feel free to stop in and check what's going on; then return to the trail and turn right onto the footbridge for King Cole Way.

The next leg takes you along the eastern edge of Riverfront Park, which served as the site of Expo '74 (the 1974 world's fair) and was built on the site of Spokane's former rail yard. The iconic clock tower from the old depot still stands to this day, just off to the left from the trail. Feel free to linger here and enjoy a picnic lunch, or perhaps let your dogs loose to play. When ready, continue up the trail as it bends to the right, past the pavilion. Continue over the next footbridge.

The bridge affords a gorgeous view of the Upper Falls and the dam just above. This makes a great spot for taking pictures and witnessing the might of Mother Nature. Once across the bridge, at a little more than 1 mile in, take a right at the Centennial Hotel and head east back toward the Gonzaga campus.

The return route continues to follow the river closely, though being across from downtown proper, it lacks the frequent art displays of the westbound leg on the south side of the river. Nevertheless, the river views are every bit as pleasant, and there's plenty of greenery to enjoy. Be mindful of bike traffic and joggers as you continue along the trail. You'll know you're getting close to the trailhead when you pass the sprawling Ruby River Hotel on your left at 1.4 miles, followed by Gonzaga's Jundt Art Museum at 1.6 miles. Eventually, you'll be able to make out the Centennial Trail bridge on the right, marking your point of origin for this hike. Continue left past the bridge and back toward the parking area.

Nearby Attractions

This hike is within walking distance of practically everything that downtown Spokane has to offer. From artistic and sporting events at Gonzaga University to the lush spaces of Riverfront Park to numerous dining options, you're sure to find something to enjoy. Be sure to check out local institutions like **Auntie's Bookstore** (auntiesbooks.com) and **Boots Bakery** (bootsbakery.com), both just a few minutes away on foot. At Riverfront Park, cable car rides afford breathtaking vistas of the city's signature bridges and Spokane Falls. If you're skittish about heights, fear not—the views are just as lovely from the various nearby overlooks, located safely on terra firma.

Directions

From downtown Spokane, take Division Street north across the Spokane River; then follow the bend to the right onto North Ruby Street. After four blocks, turn right (east) onto East Sharp Avenue; in 0.6 mile, turn right (south) onto North Hamilton Street. In 0.4 mile, turn right onto East Springfield Avenue, and then make another quick right onto North Cincinnati Street and the Gonzaga University campus. About 400 feet ahead, just after the Centennial Trail crosses the road, bear left into the large parking area—try to find a spot adjacent to or north of the School of Law building.

THE GONZAGA UNIVERSITY CAMPUS, VIEWED FROM THE SOUTH BANK OF THE SPOKANE RIVER

Spokane Valley

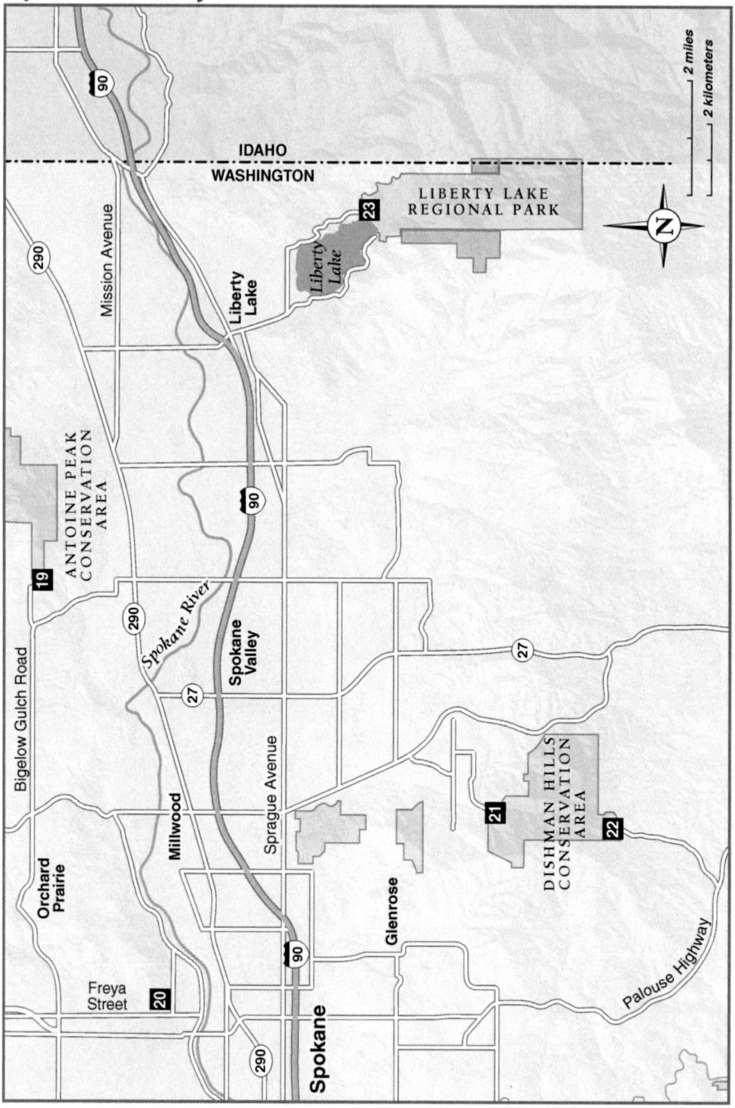

Spokane Valley

BIG ROCK OVERLOOK, DISHMAN HILLS (SEE HIKE 22, PAGE 134)
photographed by Elizabeth Marlin

19 Antoine Peak Conservation Area: Tower Road, Antoine's Summit, and Emerald Necklace

SCENERY: ★ ★ ★ ★ ★
TRAIL CONDITION: ★ ★ ★ ★
CHILDREN: ★ ★ ★
DIFFICULTY: ★ ★ ★
SOLITUDE: ★ ★ ★ ★ ★

LOOKING SOUTHWEST, BACK TOWARD SPOKANE, FROM ANTOINE'S PEAK

GPS TRAILHEAD COORDINATES: N47° 43.306' W117° 11.709'

DISTANCE & CONFIGURATION: 4.8-mile balloon

HIKING TIME: 1.5 hours

HIGHLIGHTS: Views of Green Bluff, Spokane Valley, and Dishman Hills

ELEVATION: 2,648' at lowest point, 3,358' at highest

ACCESS: Daily, 6 a.m.–10 p.m. (best attempted October–April); no fees or permits

MAPS: USGS *Greenacres, WA*; PDF map at the website below

FACILITIES: Gravel parking lot at Brevier Road

WHEELCHAIR ACCESS: No

COMMENTS: Dogs must be leashed. The trailhead for this hike is unmarked; the trail itself is generally well groomed, but not all turnouts are clearly indicated.

CONTACTS: Spokane County Parks, Recreation & Golf, 509-447-4730, spokanecounty.org/facilities/facility /details/antoine-peak-conservation-area-58

Overview

This out-of-the way hike lies in Spokane's Green Bluff region, rising above the surrounding farmlands to provide a commanding view of the entire Spokane Valley. On a clear day, you can see from Post Falls across the Idaho border and all the way east to Spokane and even Cheney. Though this hike is midrange in difficulty due to its distance and altitude gain, its slopes are gentle. It's suitable for a wide variety of ages and skill levels, with broad trails and lovely scenery.

Route Details

From the southeast corner of the parking area on Brevier Road, you'll find trails heading left (east) and straight (south)—both will get you to the start of this hike, but the trail heading straight is more direct.

In about 400 feet, turn left (east) onto Tower Road to begin the hike. The trail here consists of broad, flat-packed, sandy soil; forest cover is abundant, consisting mostly of Engelmann spruce, Douglas-fir, ponderosa pine, and the occasional western larch. Though traffic is minimal, you may occasionally encounter the odd backpacker, dog walker, or cyclist.

After about 0.6 mile, the trail winds upward and to the right, following an aggressive hairpin curve, and in another 0.2 mile the trail forks. The left path, Antoine's Summit Trail, offers a steadier uphill grade, with dense forest cover, while the right path, the Emerald Necklace Trail, is a more up-and-down route with wooded meadows and a clear view of the Spokane Valley. Regardless of which route you choose, each leads back to the trailhead, so for the purposes of this hike, take the left fork up to Antoine Peak.

The next leg of the hike follows the ridge directly up the side of the mountain. Grades will continue to be gentle and consistent. About 0.5 mile from the previous fork, you come to a second one. Going left on the Emerald Necklace Trail takes you around the north-facing side of the ridge and, as before, offers a gentler incline. For the purposes of this hike, turn right onto Antoine's Summit Trail, which affords a marginally steeper incline but also stunning views of the Spokane River valley, along with access to a few scenic overlooks that would make for ideal picnic spots.

In another 0.4 mile, just past a radio tower on your right, you reach yet another fork: Antoine's Summit Trail, to the left, takes you up to the summit of Antoine Peak, about 0.1 mile farther and marked by more radio towers.

Antoine Peak Conservation Area:
Tower Road, Antoine's Summit, and Emerald Necklace

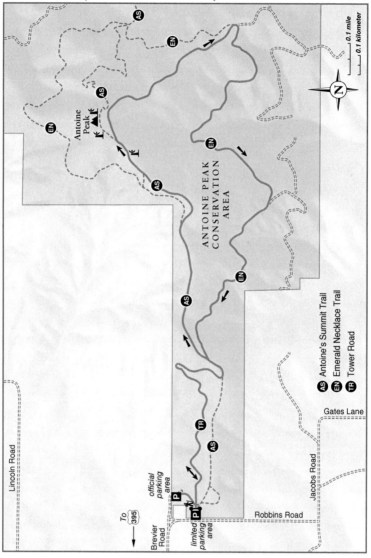

However, the views aren't appreciably better than the ones here at the fork, plus you'd have to backtrack, as Antoine's Summit Trail continues east. Instead, take the right path onto a cutoff trail that curves south about 1.8 miles from the trailhead. A word of caution: This turnoff is unmarked and easy to miss.

In this southeasterly stretch, the tree cover becomes sparser, giving way to high grassland and isolated stands of pine. After roughly 0.5 mile, the trail intersects a fire road—follow this to the right, but don't continue beyond the sign marked FIRE ACCESS. Rather, take another right at the marker onto the Emerald Necklace Trail to begin the journey home.

Where the initial segment skirted the ridge above, this return leg hugs a series of saddles and draws. The trail is also much more uneven, winding up and down, though the curves aren't terribly extreme. At about 3.25 miles, the route curves right (northwest) on its way back to where you close the loop, about 0.75 mile farther. Now back at the first fork you encountered, bear left onto the balloon string, Tower Road, and follow it back to the trailhead.

Directions

From Monroe Street in downtown Spokane, take I-90 eastbound and, after 9.2 miles, take Exit 289 onto northbound WA 27/North Pines Road. In 1.2 miles, turn right (east) onto WA 290/East Trent Avenue; then, in 1.8 miles, turn left (north) onto North Progress Road. In 1 mile, the road forks—where Progress Road veers left, continue straight (north) onto North Forker Road. In another mile, bear right at the fork to stay on North Forker Road, make another quick right at another fork to stay on this road, and then make a sharp right to continue east onto North Brevier Road. In 0.7 mile, the road forks again—continue straight and, just past the intersection, turn right into the trailhead parking area. *Note:* If you turn right (south) at the intersection onto North Robbins Road, another, more direct trailhead access is on the left in just 0.05 mile, but parking is extremely limited here, and you have to go around a locked gate to get to the trail.

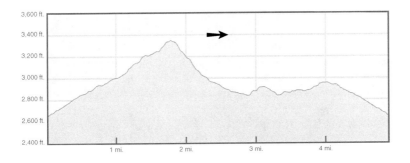

20 Beacon Hill Bike Park Loop

SCENERY: ★ ★ ★ ★
TRAIL CONDITION: ★ ★ ★ ★ ★
CHILDREN: ★ ★ ★
DIFFICULTY: ★ ★ ★
SOLITUDE: ★ ★

THE CRISSCROSSING BIKE PATHS OF BEACON HILL

GPS TRAILHEAD COORDINATES: N47° 41.283' W117° 21.092'

DISTANCE & CONFIGURATION: 2.9-mile loop

HIKING TIME: 1 hour

HIGHLIGHTS: Dense forest cover, views of the entire Spokane Valley

ELEVATION: 2,001' at lowest point, 2,604' at highest

ACCESS: Daily, 6 a.m.–11 p.m.; no fees or permits

MAPS: USGS *Spokane NE, WA*; PDF and interactive maps at evergreeneast.org/trails/campsekanibeaconhill

FACILITIES: Information board at trailhead; limited parking

WHEELCHAIR ACCESS: No

COMMENTS: Dogs must be leashed. Given the mixed-use nature of these trails, be alert to mountain bikers coming downhill at high speeds. Also note that the trail system encompasses both public land and private property, so please don't stray from the route described.

CONTACTS: Spokane City Parks and Recreation, 509-625-6200, my.spokanecity.org/parksrec; Spokane County Parks, Recreation & Golf, 509-447-4730, spokanecounty.org/1383/parks; Evergreen Mountain Bike Alliance, Eastern Washington Chapter, evergreeneast.org

Overview

Located near the boundary between Spokane and Spokane Valley, this hike is close to town and offers amazing vistas spanning the entire region. Of moderate range and difficulty, it can be attempted by active hikers of all ages; however, it sees heavy use by cyclists, and the power lines and cell towers at the summit somewhat mar the view.

Route Details

Begin from the trailhead on Bridgeport Avenue, marked by a pair of striped posts. The trail at its outset rises gently to the left, following an S-curve northeast. As you round the upper bend, make note of the shed and the parked vehicles to your left (north): this spot can serve as a suitable alternative trailhead but is mainly geared to cyclists. The information board lacks the customary county parks information, containing instead visual guides to the trail itself, as well as indicators of public versus private lands—this route traverses both.

In 0.1 mile the trail forks slightly after cresting a small embankment; for the purposes of this hike, take the rightmost fork for the southern leg. This takes you up a steep but well-graded and reasonably straight doubletrack access road, passing two trail junctions in short succession at about 0.2 mile. Numerous overlooks afford striking views of the greater Spokane area. Be sure to pace yourself during this section; though there are no designated rest areas, the overlooks provide opportunities aplenty to catch your breath and hydrate. Snap a few photos while you're at it—the afternoon light in spring is especially favorable.

At about 0.3 mile, where the access road heads left, continue straight (east), passing power lines and an electrical tower to your right. The tree cover thins quickly as you ascend the center of a wide draw. At a little less than 0.5 mile, at a fork, continue straight. The path continues upward and generally northeast.

At 0.6 mile, just past a three-way intersection, turn right to head east then southeast. Make note of yet another overlook to your right (south), 0.75 mile from the trailhead. After an additional 0.25 mile, the path diverges again, but keep left this time. By now you should have a clear view of the summit, which hosts a communications array that includes a transformer station as well as cell and radio towers.

Beacon Hill Bike Park Loop

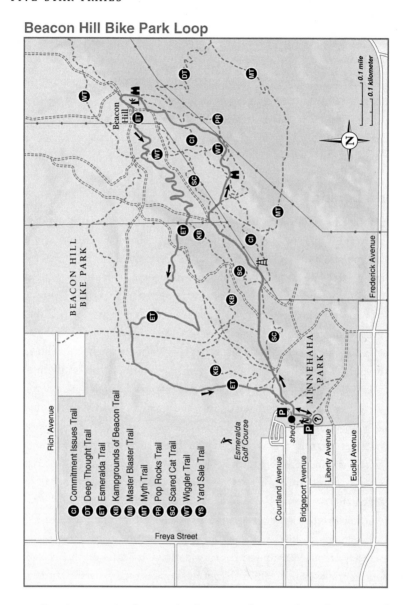

Rich Avenue

BEACON HILL BIKE PARK

Beacon Hill

MINNEHAHA PARK

Esmeralda Golf Course

shed

Courtland Avenue

Bridgeport Avenue

Liberty Avenue

Euclid Avenue

Frederick Avenue

Freya Street

0.1 mile
0.1 kilometer

CI Commitment Issues Trail
DT Deep Thought Trail
ET Esmeralda Trail
KB Kampgrounds of Beacon Trail
MB Master Blaster Trail
MT Myth Trail
PR Pop Rocks Trail
SC Scared Cat Trail
WT Wiggler Trail
YS Yard Sale Trail

Despite extensive human development, the view from the summit has much to recommend it. On a clear day, you can see all the way to Sunset Hill in the west, with a clear glimpse of the Spokane skyline. To the south are Spokane Valley and the Dishman Hills, with Mica Peak and Liberty Lake visible to the southeast. Of particular note is Felts Field, the local private airstrip, directly below you to the south at the base of the hill. For those with even a passing interest in aviation, this overlook presents a perfect spot to catch a bird's-eye view of planes taking off and landing. When you're ready, continue north up the path, which leads directly through the scattered buildings of the communications array. Please obey all posted safety warnings, as live voltage is a serious risk.

From here, the transition to the downhill leg can be a bit of a challenge, as the summit is crisscrossed by bike trails. For the moment, stay on the double-track as it hooks sharply left (southwest); then, when the path splits off roughly 200 feet farther at 1.2 miles, bear slightly right (west-southwest) onto the Esmeralda Trail.

As you descend, the route transitions back to dense forest cover and a narrow, hard-packed dirt trail, marked by numerous switchbacks. As shown by the tire tracks, this section also serves as a bike trail. Keep an ear open for whirring gears and the calls of cyclists warning of their approach. Standard trail etiquette dictates that cyclists yield to pedestrians, but be aware that bikers may not always pay heed.

At 1.4 miles, still on the Esmeralda Trail, you come to a dry streambed. It's easy to confuse this for a turn in the path, as the trail on the other bank becomes less visible in the undergrowth, but stay the course by crossing the stream. You soon come to a second set of switchbacks, beginning with a sharp hairpin turn to the right—follow it and enjoy a picturesque view to the north as you come to a break in the trees.

Continue to follow the Esmeralda Trail as it curves around to the left; as you descend, the trail once again grows broader, comfortably accommodating

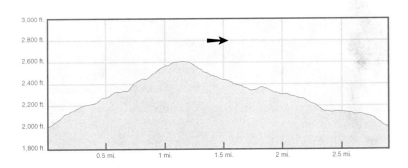

both hikers and cyclists. At 1.7 miles you cross an access road and once again pass under power lines, and in another 0.1 mile you cross another access road.

At 2.25 miles turn left (west), and at 2.4 miles, at the intersection with the Yard Sale Trail, turn left (south) to stay on Esmeralda. Keep straight (south) past two more trail intersections, and close the loop at about 2.75 miles. Soon you pass the cyclist parking area and shed that you passed back at the beginning, now on your right. Then continue down the S-curve to emerge back at the trailhead.

Directions

From Monroe Street in downtown Spokane, take I-90 eastbound. In 3 miles, take Exit 283B and turn left (north) onto North Freya Street/North Freya Way; in another 1.3 miles, follow the curve left and then right as Freya becomes North Greene Street. In 0.6 mile, shortly after crossing the Spokane River, turn right onto East Carlisle Avenue, follow it four blocks, and then turn left (north) back onto North Freya Street. In 0.6 mile, turn right (east) onto East Bridgeport Avenue, and follow it 0.3 mile until it dead-ends on a residential street just outside of the western edge of Minnehaha Park. The trailhead is marked by a pair of striped poles just beyond the tree line. A second trailhead with additional parking is located a block north, at the end of East Courtland Avenue, but it's primarily for bicyclists.

GLANCING BACK UPSLOPE ON THE LOOP'S DOWNWARD LEG

Dishman Hills Conservation
Area: Iller Creek Loop

SCENERY: ★ ★ ★ ★ ★
TRAIL CONDITION: ★ ★ ★ ★ ★
CHILDREN: ★ ★ ★
DIFFICULTY: ★ ★ ★
SOLITUDE: ★ ★ ★

A VIEW OF THE PALOUSE DURING FIRE SEASON

GPS TRAILHEAD COORDINATES: N47° 36.105' W117° 16.908'

DISTANCE & CONFIGURATION: 4.8-mile loop

HIKING TIME: 2–3 hours

HIGHLIGHTS: Excellent summer trail conditions, Rocks of Sharon overlook, views of the Palouse

ELEVATION: 2,387' at lowest point, 3,575' at highest

ACCESS: Daily, 6 a.m.–10 p.m.; no fees or permits. Though the conservation area is technically open year-round, note that many areas are blocked by snowfall in winter.

MAPS: USGS *Spokane SE, WA*; PDF maps at the website below and dishmanhills.org/maps. Also at trailhead.

FACILITIES: Portable toilet, trash can, pet-waste bags, and map board at trailhead; limited parking

WHEELCHAIR ACCESS: No

COMMENTS: Dogs must be leashed; hikers share the trail with cyclists. Bring a camera for capturing this trail's scenic views, as well as a picnic lunch to enjoy beneath the shadows of the Rocks of Sharon.

CONTACTS: Spokane County Parks, Recreation & Golf, 509-447-4730, tinyurl.com/dishman-hills; Dishman Hills Conservancy, 509-598-0003, dishmanhills.org

Dishman Hills Conservation Area: Iller Creek Loop

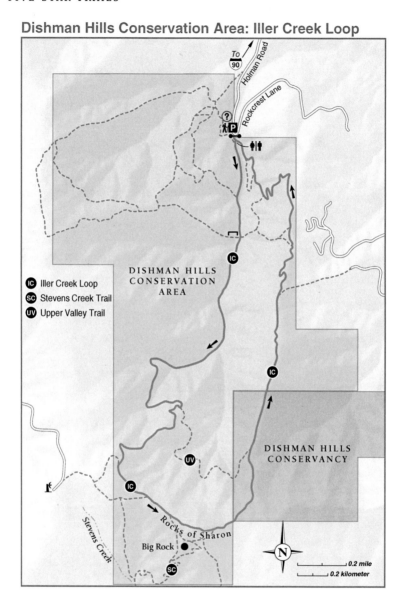

Overview

This hike is popular with pedestrians and mountain bikers across a range of skill levels. Its well-maintained trails and dense forests offer enough seclusion for solitary hikers to find their bliss. The Rocks of Sharon scenic overlook affords stunning vistas of the Spokane Valley to the north, Mica Peak to the east, and the rolling plains of the Palouse region to the south.

Route Details

This hike is somewhat off the beaten path, requiring visitors to navigate a series of winding streets through tucked-away residential subdivisions. The trailhead itself is a signed turnoff with a gate; a portable toilet and a dispenser with dog-waste bags are located just past the gate. The route described here runs counterclockwise.

Take the right fork of the Iller Creek Loop, heading south and up along the winding, narrow footpath. About 100 feet past the gate, continue straight past a map board on your right; then, in a little more than 0.25 mile, bear left at an unmarked junction. The route adjoins a streambed on the right, and travelers will find themselves enclosed by dense woodland cover. The path itself is well maintained, though narrow, and visitors should be prepared to share the route with others. Cyclists are a common sight during summer; yield and show proper courtesy as necessary. Hikers should pace themselves, as the route averages a 6–7% grade. Be sure to hydrate, taking breaks as necessary, and pay attention to the signposts placed periodically along the trail.

The path will narrow and the grade will steepen as you ascend, so don't be afraid to take breaks as needed (you'll pass a bench to your right [west] at about 0.4 mile, or about 0.1 mile from the previous junction). As you climb higher, you'll find wildflowers in full bloom in summer, among them wild thistle and mustard. Deciduous tree cover eventually gives way to evergreens, and switchbacks become common.

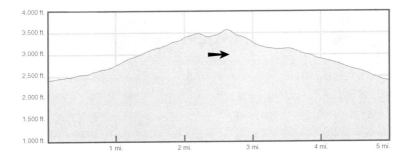

HEADING UPHILL ON ILLER CREEK LOOP

At about 0.8 mile, the trail swings right (west) and then, about 0.3 mile farther, makes a hairpin turn left and then right, continuing south. In another 0.1 mile, the trail bends sharply left (east) before entering another hairpin turn to the right (south) another 0.1 mile later. Just past this turn, at roughly the 1.5-mile mark, the trail forks again at a signed junction. Heading left (southeast) puts you on the Upper Valley Trail, forgoing the Rocks of Sharon overlook and shaving more than a mile off the route. For this hike, however, take a sharp right to head north and then southwest up the ridge and on to the rocks themselves.

After another mile, you finally clear the treeline, and you'll be high enough for a view of the entire valley, with the Rocks of Sharon visible near the summit. On a clear day you can also catch glimpses of Tower Mountain and Mica Peak to the east, the Spokane River valley and Mount Spokane to the north, and the Selkirk Mountains along the Washington–Idaho border, so have those cameras ready.

The tree cover becomes much sparser as you near Big Rock, the largest of the Rocks of Sharon. Glance right for a stunning view of the Dishman Hills and the Palouse opening up to the south. There is a signed junction with the Stevens Creek Trail (see next hike), which heads right (south), at the outcrop; here hikers can pause for a photo or a picnic or continue following the Iller Creek Loop to the left (east) toward the loop's return leg. Personally, I find this a perfect spot to enjoy a snack and take a few photos of the prairie.

Tarry at the outcrop for as long as you like; then saunter back to the trail marker and continue right (east). The grade becomes gentler through this section and continues that way for the remainder of the hike. The other Rocks of Sharon come into view at about 2.5 miles. Here are more promising picnic spots, as well as a gravel area for cyclists looking to take a break; here also are the most picturesque views of the Palouse, with its rolling hills and seas of grain. Continue on, and at about 2.7 miles the trail bends left (north) and begins its return route to the trailhead. At 3 miles, you pass a signed junction with the Upper Valley Trail to your left.

This section provides a gentle descent for those whose knees may have been tested by the climb. Be prepared for views back across the draw you ascended, as well as a sweeping panorama of Spokane to the north. Switchbacks are more frequent and cyclists more common in this stretch, but here the trail is at its widest and the soil is packed down hard. Continue back down into the woodland cover, and follow the markers as necessary. Finally, at a little more than 4.7 miles, you arrive back at the trailhead.

Directions

From Monroe Street in downtown Spokane, take I-90 eastbound. In 4.6 miles, take Exit 285 toward Sprague Avenue. In 0.6 mile, continue straight (east) onto East Appleway Boulevard; then, after 1.6 miles, turn right (south) onto South Dishman Mica Road. Continue for 2.3 miles; then turn right (southeast) onto Schafer Road. In 0.9 mile, turn right (west) onto East 44th Avenue, and in another 0.2 mile turn left (south) onto South Farr Road. In 0.3 mile, turn right (west, then south) onto East Holman Road, and follow it 0.7 mile to the Iller Creek Trailhead.

 22 Dishman Hills Conservation
Area: Stevens Creek Trail

SCENERY: ★ ★ ★ ★
TRAIL CONDITION: ★ ★ ★ ★ ★
CHILDREN: ★
DIFFICULTY: ★ ★ ★ ★
SOLITUDE: ★ ★ ★ ★

JUST PAST THE GATE, THE TRAIL'S SURFACE CHANGES FROM GRAVEL TO CRUSHED SLATE.

photographed by Elizabeth Marlin

GPS TRAILHEAD COORDINATES: N47° 34.211' W117° 17.296'

DISTANCE & CONFIGURATION: 2.0-mile out-and-back

HIKING TIME: 2.5 hours

HIGHLIGHTS: Excellent summer trail conditions, access to Big Rock, views of the Palouse

ELEVATION: 2,847' at lowest point, 3,497' at highest

ACCESS: Daily, 6 a.m.–10 p.m.; no fees or permits. Though the conservation area is technically open year-round, note that many areas are blocked by snowfall in winter.

MAPS: USGS *Spokane SE, WA*; PDF maps at the website below and dishmanhills.org/maps. Also at trailhead.

FACILITIES: Portable toilet, map board, and gravel parking lot

WHEELCHAIR ACCESS: No

COMMENTS: The trail is short but has an average grade of 12.4%, making it one of the steepest hikes in this book; therefore, it's unsuitable for kids, dogs, or anyone who isn't in reasonably good physical condition. Bring comfortable footwear and trekking poles if necessary, and expect to take things at a slow pace.

CONTACTS: Spokane County Parks, Recreation & Golf, 509-447-4730, tinyurl.com/dishman-hills; Dishman Hills Conservancy, 509-598-0003, dishmanhills.org

Overview

This hike is adjacent to a number of other trails within Dishman Hills Conservation Area, among them the Iller Creek Loop (see previous hike). Unlike these other routes, however, it must be accessed from the southern face of the Dishman Hills, via the Palouse Highway. It also culminates at the base of Big Rock, the largest formation in the Rocks of Sharon. Hikers and climbers alike will enjoy this trail, though climbers in particular should work in belay teams, as Big Rock is unsafe for bouldering or free routes. Additionally, the steep grade of this trail makes it extremely challenging for cyclists.

Route Details

This trail lies along the southern face of the Dishman Hills, and reaching it requires visitors to take a scenic drive through the prairies of the famed Palouse region. The windswept fields and rolling hills of this biome possess a distinct charm all their own, standing in stark contrast to the pines and rivers of Spokane. Just make sure not to miss the turnoff for Stevens Creek Road while you're enjoying the scenery.

The trail proper begins as soon as you leave the parking lot—be sure to consult the map board, and then turn left (north) at the TRAIL ACCESS sign to begin this brief but invigorating climb. A service gate and a trail marker lie

Dishman Hills Conservation Area: Stevens Creek Trail

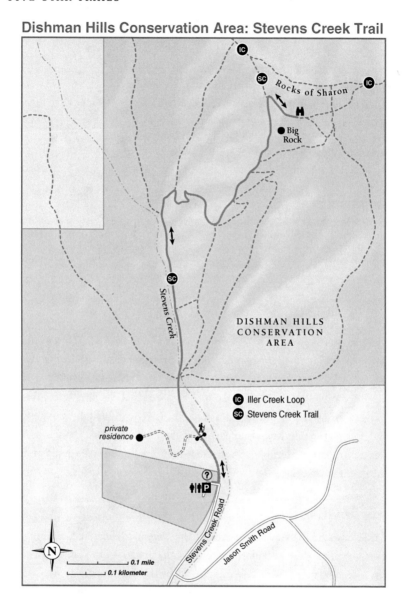

approximately 0.1 mile north up the road (the trail to the left leads to private property). Up to the gate, the trail is composed of standard gravel but transitions to crushed slate thereafter. I advise wearing closed-toe shoes for this hike, particularly in summer.

The initial leg of the trail leads through stands of pine and aspen. Even from here, hikers will be able to see Big Rock—the defining feature of this trail—towering overhead to the north. Fall visitors in particular will be treated to blazing displays of color, which contrast strikingly with the view of the prairie.

At about 0.2 mile, the trail begins to rise and you enter a large, grassy clearing. Make note of the wheel ruts up the hill to the right—these mark a portion of the original trail, which goes straight up the hill and which, while still accessible, is far more intense. Follow the current trail slightly left for a vigorous but more manageable experience.

You'll pass many trail junctions, but continue straight (north). At about 0.5 mile, you reach two junctions in quick succession; at the first, your route continues northeast, and at the second, your path veers south. Here the grade steepens and you encounter a series of small switchbacks, put in place by the Washington Trails Association to make the trail more accessible. In spite of these improvements, however, it's still prudent to use canes or trekking poles as necessary. What this hike lacks in distance, it makes up for in incline.

After a few zigs and zags up the hill, the trail widens again. At a junction at 0.7 mile, head left (north) up the hill, in the direction of Big Rock. From here, the hike is much more straightforward, but it's also its most challenging. Don't hesitate to stop and take breaks as needed—remember, a slow pace is a safe pace, and injuries on a grade of this intensity can be difficult to manage.

Before long the shadow of Big Rock looms directly overhead—at 0.9 mile, head right (southeast) up the hill at the junction. The trail continues around the formation itself, and the best views await still higher up the hill. A note regarding Big Rock: this volcanic basalt formation represents the largest in the Rocks

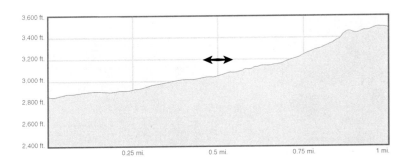

of Sharon, towering 230 feet above the surrounding terrain. As such, it constitutes a popular spot for hikers as well as rock-climbing enthusiasts. On one visit
alone, I encountered three separate belay teams making ascents. Be sure to give
climbers a wide berth for the safety of everyone involved.

From the top of the hill, looking south the way you came, you have a commanding view of the Palouse, as well as of Tower Mountain off to the right. On
clear days, you can even see the massive rise of Steptoe Butte, some 38 miles
distant. Feel free to linger and catch your breath, snap photos, or enjoy a picnic.
When you're ready, return the way you came; you could also go right (north) at
the first junction on your way back from the overlook to join the Iller Creek Loop
(see previous hike). Whatever option you choose, you won't be disappointed.

Directions

From Monroe Street in downtown Spokane, take I-90 eastbound. After 2.8 miles,
take Exit 283B for Thor Street/Freya Street. In 0.2 mile, merge onto East Third
Avenue; then, in another 0.1 mile, turn right (south) onto South Thor Street.
After 0.5 mile, turn left (east) onto East 11th Avenue; then, in 0.1 mile, right
(south) onto South Freya Street. Drive 2.7 miles, and then turn left (south) onto
South Palouse Highway. After 5.9 miles, turn left (northeast) onto South Stevens Creek Road and follow it an additional 2.2 miles, at which point the signed
parking lot for the Stevens Creek Trailhead will be visible on the left.

THIS HIKE IS SHORT BUT STRENUOUS DUE TO ITS STEEP GRADE.   photographed by Elizabeth Marlin

SCENERY: ★ ★ ★ ★ ★
TRAIL CONDITION: ★ ★ ★ ★ ★
CHILDREN: ★ ★
DIFFICULTY: ★ ★ ★ ★ ★
SOLITUDE: ★ ★ ★ ★

IMPROVISED LOG BRIDGE ON THE LIBERTY LAKE LOOP TRAIL

GPS TRAILHEAD COORDINATES: N47° 37.854' W117° 03.508'

DISTANCE & CONFIGURATION: 8.2-mile loop

HIKING TIME: 3–4 hours

HIGHLIGHTS: Liberty Creek Wetlands Reclamation Area, Cedar Grove Conservation Area, waterfalls, optional hiking loop of 4 miles at turnaround point, camping

ELEVATION: 2,059' at lowest point, 3,293' at highest

ACCESS: Daily, 6 a.m.–10 p.m. Best during late summer or early autumn, as heavy snowfall persists at higher altitudes October–June. From the Friday before Memorial Day–Labor Day, a $2 day-use fee (payable at the entrance booth) is charged Monday–Thursday, 8 a.m.–5 p.m., and Friday–Sunday, 8 a.m.–7 p.m.

MAPS: USGS *Liberty Lake* and *Mica Peak, WA;* PDF maps at the website on the next page

FACILITIES: Restrooms, playground, swimming beach, picnic pavilion, map board, parking, and campground near trailhead

WHEELCHAIR ACCESS: No

Liberty Lake Loop Trail

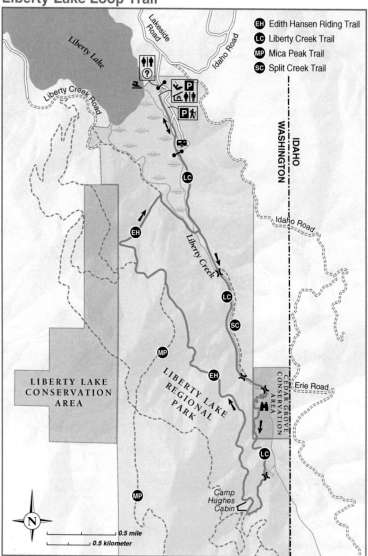

COMMENTS: Dogs must be leashed. Cell service is limited, so carrying a dedicated GPS unit and hiking with a partner are strongly advised. Sightings of wildlife, including bears and elk, are common. Because of its distance and elevation gain, this hike is not recommended for very young children or anyone not in reasonably good physical condition.

CONTACTS: Liberty Lake Regional Park, 509-255-6861, spokanecounty.org/facilities/facility/details /liberty-lake-regional-park-39

Overview

This mountain hike takes you through a stretch of reclaimed wetlands before ascending through cedar forests to a stunning waterfall view. At slightly more than 8 miles round-trip, with a 1,300-foot altitude gain, the Liberty Lake Loop Trail is one of the book's most challenging hikes; it also offers plenty of solitude if crowds aren't your thing.

Route Details

Liberty Lake has two day-use parking areas: a paved lot just past the entry booth, as well as a smaller dirt lot about 0.2 mile farther south; both, however, are 0.25–0.5 mile from the beginning of the trail proper. A dirt pathway leads south from the first parking area, past the second parking area, and then past the RV camping area and restroom facilities on the left, to a portable toilet and map board. Proceed past the service gate.

The ascent in this section is gentle and fairly straightforward, hewing close to the path carved out by Liberty Creek. Pay special attention to the wetlands on the right, keeping an eye out for information boards on this fascinating transitional ecosystem. Beaver dams are common throughout this stretch, but remember to avoid disturbing the local wildlife or their dwellings.

About 0.4 mile past the service gate, you reach a T-junction. The hike described here runs clockwise, but for a less intense climb, you can go counterclockwise by turning right (northwest) onto the signed Edith Hansen Riding Trail. This makes for a somewhat gentler ascent overall, although horses share

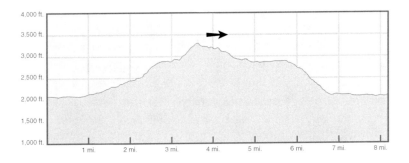

the trail with hikers here. Otherwise, continue straight (south) toward the Liberty Creek Cedar Grove.

About 0.3 mile ahead, you reach another junction. The left fork leads you onto the Split Creek Trail, which heads south about 1 mile, paralleling the Liberty Creek Trail on the east side of the stream, before rejoining the main Liberty Creek Trail to form a narrow loop (think a really deflated balloon). For this hike, though, bear right across a wooden footbridge over Liberty Creek. At about 2 miles, you cross a second footbridge just before the Split Creek Trail merges from the left.

About 0.15 mile farther, you reach the Liberty Creek Cedar Grove Conservation Area. As noted on the accompanying information board, the grove was purchased in 1987 and has since been maintained as a space for rest and reflection for hikers. Take a moment to snap some photos and perhaps rest up on the nearby bench; then, about 370 feet farther, cross yet another footbridge off to your right.

Past this footbridge, the trail's difficulty escalates as the grade steepens into a series of punishing switchbacks, which will continue until the waterfall just before the trail's high point. Trekking poles are highly recommended, as are frequent breaks and regular hydration. Pace this section according to what feels comfortable. (A quick reminder: water and a first aid kit are essential even on very short excursions.)

The trail continues to climb steadily, at times reaching grades of 11%. Eventually you'll crest the treeline—be sure to capture a few shots looking east toward Mica Peak or north for a view of the Otis Orchards–Newman Lake area. In this section, equestrian traffic becomes more likely, though given the trail's length and difficulty, you're still less likely to encounter fellow hikers here than on other local trails. At just shy of 3.2 miles, you come to still another footbridge just below a picturesque waterfall.

The switchbacks continue past the bridge, with the same intensity of grade, leading hikers up to the mouth of the waterfall. The flow is low in late summer, but late-spring visitors can expect a breathtaking spectacle just after the snowmelt. Leaving the falls behind, you reach the hike's high point (3,293') about 0.4 mile ahead, and you soon find yourself in another secluded grove of old-growth cedar and pine.

Savor the silence and the fresh mountain air, but keep an eye out for wildlife, black bears in particular. On this hike I've spotted fresh bear droppings, which are black to purple depending on the bear's diet and which often contain the remnants of various berries and seeds. While bears are generally shy and solitary animals, mothers with cubs and territorial males can become defensive or aggressive (see page 14 for information on what to do in case of a bear encounter).

At about 3.6 miles, you come to a north–south junction—the south (left) fork is helpfully labeled with a sign that reads MORE HIKING and takes you on an optional side loop totaling 4 miles. For this hike, however, take the north (right) fork onto the Edith Hansen Riding Trail, passing the Camp Hughes Cabin on your left before you head back down the mountain.

For the return leg, the trail and its slope grow considerably gentler. The path here is broad and smooth, though it does grow rockier near the bottom of the descent. Pay attention to the signs indicating right-of-way for cyclists and horseback riders, but otherwise feel free to take this section at whatever pace you prefer. At 5.7 miles the Mica Peak Trail meets the Edith Hansen Riding Trail; continue heading north. At 6.1 miles a trail heads left (west) toward the Liberty Lake Conservation Area, but again your route continues north.

At about 6.8 miles, the elevation levels and you take a hairpin turn right (southeast); then, at just shy of 7.3 miles, you find yourself back at the junction with the Liberty Creek Trail—take a left back through the wetlands before returning at last to the trailhead at 8.2 miles.

Nearby Attractions

This trail, while a bit out of the way, boasts impressive camping facilities near the trailhead, as well as beach and playground facilities for summertime visitors. Those who've worked up an appetite are encouraged to check out the many excellent dining options back in Liberty Lake or take a quick jaunt across the Idaho border to Post Falls or Coeur d'Alene. All of these towns boast a wide variety of culinary options, ranging from traditional American fare to haute cuisine and even sushi. Whatever your preferences, this hike makes for the cornerstone of a perfect summertime getaway, far from the heat and traffic of Spokane.

Directions

From Monroe Street in downtown Spokane, take I-90 eastbound. After 15 miles, take Exit 296 for Liberty Lake/Appleway Avenue; then turn immediately right (south) onto Liberty Lake Road. In 1.1 miles, turn left (east) onto East Sprague Avenue; then, in another 1.1 miles, follow the curve right (south), at which point Sprague becomes South Neyland Avenue. In 0.8 mile, bear right across East Neyland Avenue/South Windsong Drive, and immediately bear right (south) onto South Lakeside Road; then, in 0.7 mile, bear right to continue south onto South Zephyr Road. In 0.3 mile, arrive at the entrance booth for Liberty Lake Regional Park, where you'll pay the day-use fee in season. Park either in the large lot to your right just past the booth or in a smaller lot about 0.2 mile farther south, signed TRAILHEAD PARKING and NO DAY-USE PARKING BEYOND THIS POINT. When the booth is gated (after hours or in the off-season), additional parking is available to the left of the park entrance, marked by a mailbox and a LIBERTY LAKE REGIONAL PARK sign.

HALFWAY UP THE HILL ON THE LIBERTY LAKE LOOP TRAIL

Mount Spokane State Park

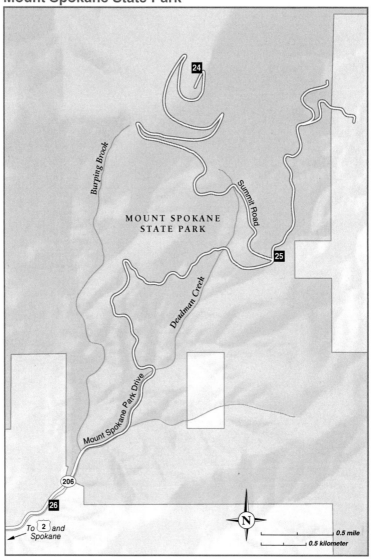

Mount Spokane State Park

WOODLAND DESCENT ON TRAIL 100 IN MOUNT SPOKANE STATE PARK
(SEE HIKE 25, PAGE 155) photographed by Elizabeth Marlin

24 Mount Spokane State Park:
Summit Loop

SCENERY: ★ ★ ★ ★ ★
TRAIL CONDITION: ★ ★
CHILDREN: ★ ★
DIFFICULTY: ★ ★ ★ ★ ★
SOLITUDE: ★ ★ ★ ★

BERRY BUSHES LINE THE TRAIL IN MOUNT SPOKANE STATE PARK.

photographed by Elizabeth Marlin

GPS TRAILHEAD COORDINATES: N47° 55.360' W117° 06.809'

DISTANCE & CONFIGURATION: 4.7-mile balloon

HIKING TIME: 1.75 hours

HIGHLIGHTS: Old-growth forest, views from the summit of Mount Spokane, access to the Civilian Conservation Corps Heritage Area

ELEVATION: 4,911' at lowest point, 5,860' at highest

ACCESS: Daily, 6:30 a.m.–sunset. Depending on the season and where you park, you must buy a Washington State Parks Discover Pass ($10/day, $30/year), a Sno-Park Permit ($20/day, $40/season), and/or a Special Groomed Trails Permit ($20/day, $40/season). See mountspokane.org/img/MtSpokaneAccess2019 .pdf for details. To buy passes online, go to discoverpass.wa.gov and epermits.parks.wa.gov/store/sno /snochoice.aspx.

MAPS: USGS *Mount Spokane, WA;* Dharma Maps *Mount Spokane State Park (WA01)* (dharmamaps.com); at trailhead; PDF maps at the websites below

FACILITIES: Map board and gravel parking lot at trailhead; restrooms and map board at Vista House/Chair 1 parking area; portable toilet and rest area at Saddle Junction turnaround

WHEELCHAIR ACCESS: No

COMMENTS: Dogs must be leashed. This hike can be accessed only via Summit Road, which is closed to motor vehicles during the winter season: from mid-October to mid-June, you must park at the Lower Selkirk lot and hike 4 strenuous miles uphill along Summit Road from the bottom of the mountain. The return segment along Mount Kit Carson Lower Loop Road is shared with cars and bikes and has no shoulder, so be alert for passing vehicles. Finally, note that cell service is spotty to nonexistent in and around the park— in an emergency, go to Selkirk Lodge, which provides maps and other park information along with restrooms, water, and indoor seating. Located across the road from and 0.2 mile east of the Lower Selkirk Parking Lot, it's open daily, 7 a.m.–5 p.m., December–March.

CONTACTS: Mount Spokane State Park, 509-238-4258, parks.state.wa.us/549/mount-spokane; The Friends of Mount Spokane State Park, mountspokane.org

Overview

This hike lies within Mount Spokane State Park at the summit of Mount Spokane itself. It follows Trail 140 down into the valley between Mount Spokane and Mount Kit Carson before intersecting Summit Road, winding back through the 1934 Civilian Conservation Corps (CCC) fire-watch lookout, and finally returning to the summit. Hikers enjoy stunning views of the entire Spokane Valley, with Micah Peak, the Dishman Hills, the Lower Selkirk Mountains, and Lake Coeur d'Alene all visible on clear days. Be aware, however, that the trail has steep switchbacks and rocky trail surfaces, making for a grueling journey. The hike requires stamina and advance knowledge of the larger Mount Spokane trail network, and it's best left to serious outdoors enthusiasts and families with older children.

Mount Spokane State Park: Summit Loop

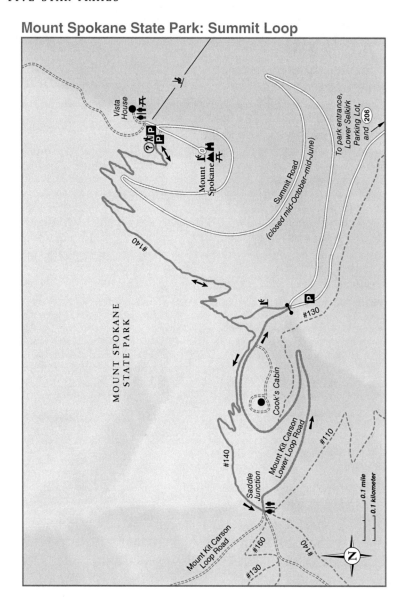

Route Details

The trailhead lies at the southwest corner of a small gravel parking lot, just west of Vista House and the Chair 1 ski-lift station. The path passes between a wooden fence on your left and a map board and signpost for Trail 140—which makes up most of the route for this trip—on the right. Look up and notice the periodic blue blazes on the trees. The trail gradually curves left and then makes a hairpin turn right (north) down into the woods, which open into a large clearing about 0.1 mile from the trailhead. The scenery improves past here, but in the meantime be sure to pause and catch a few shots of Mount Kit Carson, across the valley to the west.

A little more than 0.1 mile from the previous hairpin turn, Trail 140 makes a sharp turn left and then quickly transitions to a series of switchbacks, zigzagging generally northwest and weaving in and out between clearing and forest. The path is well defined and reasonably well maintained, but mind the buried rocks and tree roots, which are numerous and can lead to injury. Follow the switchbacks—seven in all over the course of 0.4 mile—and eventually the trail makes a hard left and opens into a lengthy downward straightaway. Follow this southwest for another 0.4 mile.

At the bottom of the straightaway, you switchback right, left, and then right over about 0.1 mile before turning left again and resuming a southwest course. In another 0.1 mile, you come to a fork. To the left is a dirt road—a service access that you can follow left (south) to return to a trailhead in an emergency. For this hike, however, keep right to continue southwest, again noting the blue-diamond trail markers affixed to the trees.

In another 0.1 mile past the fork, Trail 140 bends right (west) and passes a marker, also on the right. The next section is broad and relatively straight, hewing closely to the service road on the left (south) as it proceeds west. Then, in about 0.2 mile, comes another section of small switchbacks; here the beauty of Mount Spokane's trail system is on full display. Dense stands of spruce and fir

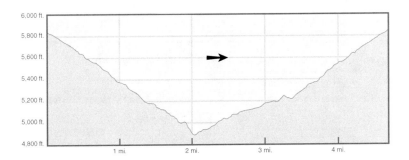

loom overhead, contrasting in fall against the blazing golds of larch as they lose their needles. The route flattens again after the switchbacks, curving gently left (southwest) for another 0.3 mile.

Eventually, a clearing in the trees appears, and just ahead you see a cylindrical portable toilet that resembles a water tank. This spot, called Saddle Junction, is the convergence of Trails 140, 130, 110, and 160; it also serves as the starting point of this loop's return leg. Take a few moments to use the facilities, check your maps, change your socks, or just plant yourself for a bit on one of the conveniently placed logs.

When you're ready to proceed, orient yourself in the clearing to find the trail: just to the left of the path on which you emerged from the woods, find the signpost–kiosk reading SADDLE JUNCTION: EXPECT DESCENDING BICYCLE TRAFFIC. Facing away from the signpost, with the MT. KIT CARSON sign directly in front of you across the clearing and the portable toilet off to the left of that, rotate to your left until you see the very leftmost trail (the trail marker, also off to the left, has nine vertically stacked icons). Head straight (west) on this trail, Mount Kit Carson Lower Loop Road.

This next leg of the journey is relatively smooth, with a gentle incline, but please be mindful of both bicycle and car traffic. About 0.5 mile ahead, follow the hairpin turn left (west), passing a junction with Trail 130 to your right about 0.2 mile farther. About 0.1 mile after this junction, as the trail begins to curve to the right (east), look for signs on the right marking the park's CCC Heritage Area. This location was historically the summer camp for Company 949 of the Civilian Conservation Corps (CCC), which maintained the park and local fire-watch station during the Great Depression. Take a few minutes to wander around, snap a few photos, or take a load off inside the CCC-built woodshed and warming hut, also known as Cook's Cabin, off the trail to the right. The rustic structure was named in honor of Francis Cook, an early-20th-century Spokane newspaperman and real estate developer who once owned 320 acres of land in what is now the state park. In 1909 Cook built the first road to the summit of what was then known variously as Mount Baldy and Mount Carlton (Cook renamed it Mount Spokane in 1913); he also built a rustic mountaintop resort called Paradise Camp where today's CCC Heritage Area stands.

When your appetite for history is sated, return to the service road, hang a right, and continue east about 0.5 mile until you reach a service gate; then follow the hairpin turn left (north). After a few hundred yards, you'll spy a small transmission tower up ahead and to the right, indicating the point at which the road appears to dead-end at a service shed. Fear not, though; you're still on the right track. Off to the left are a small concrete platform and a walkway leading down and to the north—pay attention here, as this turnoff is easily missed and the trail is difficult to locate again should you get lost.

About 0.1 mile past the transmission tower, you close the loop back at the initial fork in the trail, where you turn right to begin the long wind back up the mountain. As you continue up the switchbacks (using trekking poles if needed), allow yourself frequent breaks and drink plenty of water. After a final

WILDFLOWERS BORDER THE PATH IN SPRING. photographed by Elizabeth Marlin

push through the woods, the incline tapers off, and you find yourself back at the trailhead at just shy of 4.7 miles.

Nearby Attractions

This route is close to several other trails within Mount Spokane State Park, including Trails 110, 100, 130, and 160, and is just a short drive from the orchards, meaderies, and country boutiques of the **Green Bluff** agricultural area. It's also a popular winter destination for snowshoers, snowmobilers, and cross-country skiers; downhill aficionados can also find fresh powder at the park's Alpine ski area. Nearby dining options include **Chaney's Bottoms-Up Inn** (509-238-9188) and **Bear Creek Lodge** (bearcreeklodgewa.com). **Green Bluff Grange 300**, out on Greenbluff Road, hosts weekend pancake socials spring–fall; check its Facebook page (tinyurl.com/greenbluffgrange300) for more information.

Directions

From Monroe Street in downtown Spokane, take I-90 eastbound. After roughly 7 miles, take Exit 287 left (north) onto North Mullan Road, which becomes North Argonne Road after 0.1 mile and then North Bruce Road 6.1 miles after that. In another 2.3 miles, take the first exit off the traffic circle right (east) onto WA 206/East Mount Spokane Park Drive, which switchbacks generally northeast. (*Note:* Past the traffic circle, cell coverage becomes unreliable to nonexistent.) After about 13.4 miles (0.4 mile past Bear Creek Lodge on your left), you reach the gated park entrance and a ranger station on your left—if you didn't buy your park passes online, you'll need to stop in here (if the office is closed, pay at the automated fee station outside). Then, 1 mile ahead on your left, you reach a sign for the Kit Carson Lower Loop Road—here, follow the hairpin curve around to the right (east). After an additional 2 miles, turn left (north) onto North Summit Road. (*Note:* The turnoff is gated mid-October to mid-June—in this case, you'll need to continue straight, park in the lot just across the road on the right, walk back to the turnoff, and then follow the remaining directions on foot.) In another 1.7 miles, make a sharp right to continue on Summit Road, and follow the switchbacks west and east for 2.1 more miles. Finally, just past a large paved parking lot on your right at the top of the road, park in a smaller gravel lot, also on your right, just before the road bends south and dead-ends at the summit of Mount Spokane.

Mount Spokane State Park:
Trail 100

TREES SHADE THE SUN-DAPPLED PATH. photographed by Elizabeth Marlin

SCENERY: ★ ★ ★
TRAIL CONDITION: ★ ★ ★ ★ ★
CHILDREN: ★ ★ ★
DIFFICULTY: ★ ★ ★ ★
SOLITUDE: ★ ★ ★ ★

GPS TRAILHEAD COORDINATES: N47° 54.276' W117° 06.184'

DISTANCE & CONFIGURATION: 3.0-mile out-and-back or 1.5-mile point-to-point

HIKING TIME: 1–2.2 hours

HIGHLIGHTS: Old-growth forest, berry picking in summer

ELEVATION: 4,002' at lowest point, 4,657' at highest

ACCESS: Daily, 6:30 a.m.–sunset. Depending on the season and where you park, you must buy a Washington State Parks Discover Pass ($10/day, $30/year), a Sno-Park Permit ($20/day, $40/season), and/or a Special Groomed Trails Permit ($20/day, $40/season). See mountspokane.org/img/MtSpokaneAccess2019 .pdf for details. To buy passes online, go to discoverpass.wa.gov and epermits.parks.wa.gov/store/sno /snochoice.aspx.

MAPS: USGS *Mount Spokane, WA*; Dharma Maps *Mount Spokane State Park (WA01)* (dharmamaps.com); PDF maps at the websites below; free paper maps available at Selkirk Lodge, across the road from and 0.2 mile east of the trailhead parking area

FACILITIES: Vault toilets directly across the road from the trailhead parking area; additional restrooms, water, and parking at Selkirk Lodge

Mount Spokane State Park: Trail 100

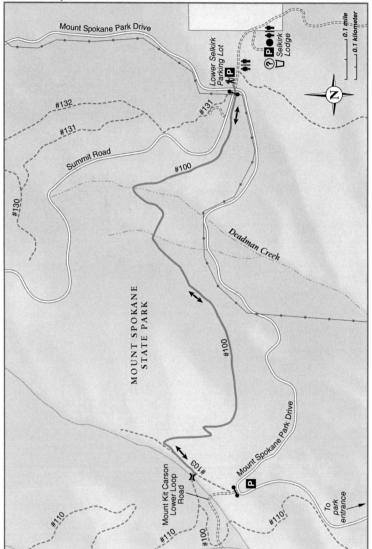

WHEELCHAIR ACCESS: No

COMMENTS: Dogs must be leashed. Hikers share the trail with cyclists and equestrians. Note that cell service is spotty to nonexistent in and around the park—in an emergency, go to Selkirk Lodge (open daily, 7 a.m.–5 p.m., December–March).

CONTACTS: Mount Spokane State Park, 509-238-4258, parks.state.wa.us/549/mount-spokane; The Friends of Mount Spokane State Park, mountspokane.org

Overview

Located on the slopes of Mount Spokane, southeast of Newport, this trail can be reached only by way of a scenic drive through the Green Bluff agricultural region. Orchards and meaderies soon give way to country roads winding through deep forest, before depositing hikers at a gravel parking area near the trailhead, from which this and multiple other trails can be enjoyed. Be advised that while cell and radio towers stud the summit of Mount Spokane overhead, the park itself lies deep within a dead zone. Guidebooks (such as this one), a dedicated GPS unit, a compass, and/or supplemental maps are recommended for those who don't know the area.

Route Details

Just across Summit Road southwest of the Lower Selkirk Parking Lot, the beginning of Trail 100 is marked by a signpost and a closed service gate. Go around the gate and follow the doubletrack straight (west) for about 0.2 mile, at which point the vehicle access gives way to a more typically narrow pedestrian trail. Note the intermittent blue blazes painted on/affixed to the trees. At about 0.4 mile, the trail hooks sharply left (south)—from this point the gentle rise on this portion of the route transitions to a downward slope, which continues from here until the turnaround.

Note that Trail 100 isn't for hikers only: mountain bikers often zip past, and the occasional pile of manure speaks to the trail's popularity with equestrians, so pay attention to your surroundings and cede access to both cyclists and horseback riders. Never approach a horse without the express permission of its rider—skittish horses may bite or kick, endangering hikers and riders alike.

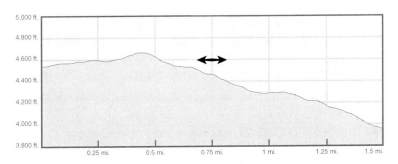

You may also encounter signs of local wildlife, which will be discussed in greater detail below.

As the trail winds downward, late-summer visitors can expect to find a tasty surprise in the form of berries ripe for the picking. When I hiked Trail 100 one early-August day, large stands of huckleberry, wild currant, and thimbleberry were coming into season. These berries can be enjoyed fresh off the bush or gathered in buckets to make pies and jams. *Note:* If you're not absolutely sure that a particular berry is safe to eat, leave it alone—a plant-identification guide would be good to bring along on this hike.

Be aware as well that the berry patches are frequented not just by humans but also the local black bears. (Their droppings, about the size of a human boot print, may be dark purple or blue if the culprit is a berry-loving bear.) These animals are generally keen to avoid humans and disinclined toward confrontation, but see page 14 for what to do if a run-in turns threatening. Report all bear encounters at Selkirk Lodge.

The downhill grade intensifies as you continue to descend. In the final 0.25 mile before the turnaround point, you'll come upon numerous switchbacks and (depending on what time of year you hike) seasonal streamlets. Tree cover is at its densest in this stretch, and in the early part of the day, the trail is well shielded from the sun. The path is wide and well maintained, and footbridges and switchbacks make the trek easier. Nevertheless, step carefully and take your time, as much to savor your surroundings as for safety's sake; likewise, pay close attention to the trail markers posted at regular intervals. Incidentally, you may find that you have sporadic cell service. As always, though, don't assume that your phone—or your GPS unit, for that matter—will work on the trail.

At just shy of 1.4 miles, Trail 100 bends left (southeast) and intersects Trail 103; a signpost marks the junction. A few yards farther, you arrive at the turnaround point, near a small footbridge on the right.

Given that up to this point the trail has trended largely downhill, the most strenuous part of the hike will be the return journey. Build in time for frequent breaks, and hydrate often, as heat-related illness is a common risk during dry, smoky Spokane summers. Fortunately, the uphill grade decreases as you draw closer to the trailhead, eventually switching over to a gentle descent.

Alternatively, you could do this hike as a point-to-point, with cars at the Lower Selkirk Parking Lot to the east and the trailhead parking area for Mount

Kit Carson Lower Loop Road to the west. In this case, instead of turning around, you would continue straight (southeast) on Trail 103, pass through a gate, and then cross Mount Spokane Park Drive to reach your shuttle vehicle.

Nearby Attractions

The state park boasts breathtaking views from the summit of Mount Spokane, which is covered in the previous hike. Two points of interest near the summit are the Depression-era **Cook's Cabin** and **Vista House** (the latter was the original site of the local fire tower). If hiking has made you work up an appetite, **Bear Creek Lodge** (bearcreeklodgewa.com), just west of the park entrance, serves homey fare at reasonable prices. Or take a scenic drive through the **Green Bluff** agricultural area, where you can pick your own fruit in season (see greenbluffgrowers .com for a list of participating farms and orchards). And **Green Bluff Grange 300**, out on Greenbluff Road, hosts weekend pancake socials spring–fall; check its Facebook page (tinyurl.com/greenbluffgrange300) for more information.

Directions

From Monroe Street in downtown Spokane, take I-90 eastbound. After roughly 7 miles, take Exit 287 left (north) onto North Mullan Road, which becomes North Argonne Road after 0.1 mile and then North Bruce Road 6.1 miles after that. In another 2.3 miles, take the first exit off the traffic circle right (east) onto WA 206/East Mount Spokane Park Drive, which switchbacks generally northeast. (*Note:* Past the traffic circle, cell coverage becomes unreliable to nonexistent.) After about 13.4 miles (0.4 mile past Bear Creek Lodge on your left), you reach the gated park entrance and a ranger station on your left—if you didn't buy your park passes online, you'll need to stop in here (if the office is closed, pay at the automated fee station outside). Then, about 1 mile ahead on your right, just before Mount Spokane Park Drive makes a hairpin turn to the right (east), you reach the trailhead parking area for Kit Carson Lower Loop Road—if you want to do this hike as a point-to-point, leave a shuttle vehicle here before continuing around the turn. After an additional 2 miles, North Summit Road veers left—continue straight and make an immediate right into the gravel parking area just across the road. The trailhead is just southwest of the parking lot, on the south side of Summit Road.

26 **Mount Spokane State Park:**
Trail 120—Bear Creek Lodge Loop

SCENERY: ★ ★ ★ ★ ★
TRAIL CONDITION: ★ ★ ★ ★
CHILDREN: ★ ★ ★
DIFFICULTY: ★ ★ ★ – ★ ★ ★ ★
SOLITUDE: ★ ★ ★ ★ ★

SUNLIT TRAIL 120

GPS TRAILHEAD COORDINATES: N47° 52.871' W117° 08.141'

DISTANCE & CONFIGURATION: 2.4-mile loop

HIKING TIME: 1 hour

HIGHLIGHTS: Dense old-growth forest, views of Mount Kit Carson

ELEVATION: 3,035' at lowest point, 3,633' at highest

ACCESS: Because the trailhead is south of the state park boundary, you don't have to buy a Discover Pass or Sno-Park Permit; you still have to pay a parking fee, however. Bear Creek Lodge, a hotel and restaurant, owns the trailhead parking lot and issues its own day-use pass for visitors who aren't staying overnight: it's $5 at the time of this writing, but check ahead to be safe (509-238-9114). *Your car will be towed if you don't have a pass.* The parking lot, just across Mount Spokane Park Drive from the lodge, is open daily, 8 a.m.–midnight.

MAPS: USGS *Foothills* and *Mount Kit Carson, WA;* Dharma Maps *Mount Spokane State Park (WA01)* (dharmamaps.com); at the websites below

FACILITIES: Gravel parking lot at trailhead (portable toilet sometimes available); restrooms and restaurant at Bear Creek Lodge

WHEELCHAIR ACCESS: No

COMMENTS: Dogs must be leashed. Hikers share the trail with cyclists and (in winter) snowmobiles. Cell coverage here is sporadic at best, and even GPS signals can be unreliable due to the rugged terrain. Navigation could be a challenge if you come unprepared.

CONTACTS: Mount Spokane State Park, 509-238-4258, parks.state.wa.us/549/mount-spokane; The Friends of Mount Spokane State Park, mountspokane.org

Overview

Located at the base of Mount Spokane and straddling the southern boundary of the state park, this secluded loop isn't as well known or heavily visited as some of its contemporaries. On the contrary, it's often overlooked even by seasoned outdoors enthusiasts, as it's mostly disconnected from the larger trail network within the park. If you arrive first thing in the morning, chances are good that you'll have the trail completely to yourself.

Over the course of just 2.4 miles, the hike packs in a steep ascent to the halfway point followed by a similarly steep descent back to the trailhead—almost 600 feet of elevation change each way. Whether you hike clockwise or counterclockwise, you're in for a pretty strenuous climb. Plus, the descent can be slippery when the ground is wet.

Older kids manage the ups and downs pretty well, but seniors will want to bring trekking poles. Experienced hikers can complete the loop in about an hour, but don't worry if it takes you longer: don't push yourself beyond your abilities, take as many breaks as you need, and stay hydrated.

Potential for pooping out aside, several aspects of this hike can be confusing when taken together. There is very little signage—of particular note, there's none at the trailhead. And even though the hike is a simple loop, with no balloon strings, figure eights, spurs, or the like, you round many curves and switchbacks along the way. Factor in heavy forest cover, little to no cell reception, no blazes on the trees, and the aforementioned scarcity of signage, and you could end up off-course if you're not paying attention. So study the route before you go, and take along supplemental navigational aids: paper maps, digital maps printed out or downloaded to your phone, guidebooks such as this one, and/or a compass.

Route Details

Go to the southernmost end of the Bear Creek Lodge parking area (on the far left if you're facing the lodge), and cross Deadman Creek on a small metal footbridge, marked with an upside-down sign reading SNOWTUBING. Exit the bridge onto the edge of a vast clearing, which in winter is used by snow tubers.

Right about now you may be asking yourself, "So where's the trail?" No signage indicates where to go or what to do next, and a quick look around doesn't readily reveal your starting point. But keep reading.

Mount Spokane State Park: Trail 120–Bear Creek Lodge Loop

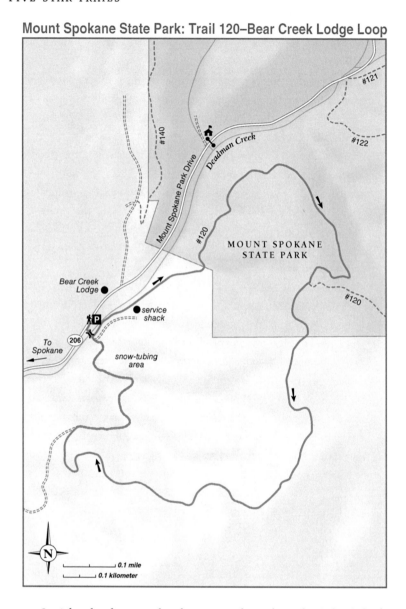

Straight ahead across the clearing is where the right fork of the loop begins—you can't see the trail from here, but you reach it by crossing the field and passing between a power-line pole on the left and a rock formation on the right.

To your immediate left, sandwiched between Deadman Creek on the left and a low, rocky, ridgelike formation to the right, is a mowed-grass alley of sorts leading straight ahead (east-northeast)—this is your starting point for a clockwise circuit. Though the trail is unsigned, online maps identify it as Trail 120.

The left fork picks up elevation gently at first on a grassy, well-maintained footpath. Note the signage for the tubing hill and the vintage farm equipment parked near the maintenance shack, on your right about 0.1 mile from the start.

Beyond this point, signs of human presence fade quickly, and the path transitions from grass to the more typical dirt and crushed rock. Another 0.1 mile or so past the service shack, the trail begins to bend to the right (east) while climbing suddenly and sharply; then, about 350 feet farther, it switchbacks left and then right as it crosses into Mount Spokane State Park.

Past the park boundary, Trail 120 continues to trend right (northeast) and pick up elevation, making a couple more switchbacks at 0.4 mile and 0.55 mile. Just past the second switchback, you reach the top of the loop—here, the trail once more bends right, now heading southeast as it continues to climb through the trees.

Pace yourself through this most strenuous stretch, as even experienced hikers in peak shape can find themselves quickly exhausted. What's more, taking your time not only helps you recover but also draws your attention to the wildflowers that grow all along the trail, from wild daisy in the spring to henbane and wild currant in summer and early fall. Savor the colors and fragrances, and perhaps sneak a few currants or thimbleberries if they're in season. Take a

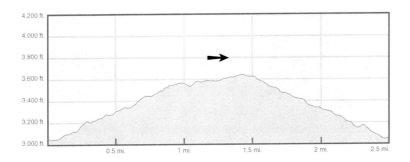

few photos as well; the hike is home to a truly awe-inspiring old-growth forest, composed chiefly of fir, larch, and cedar.

At a little more than 0.8 mile, the trail makes a sharp switchback to the right (west); about 0.7 mile later, it dips briefly downhill and then uphill. Then, just a couple hundred feet ahead, you reach a break in the trees and arrive at a junction. A sign to your left indicates the junction, but the text is on the side of the sign facing away from you as you approach. The front of the sign indicates that Trail 120 heads left (east)—for this hike, you take the right fork west and then south. What this right fork is called, however, is anybody's guess—not only is it unsigned here, it isn't labeled on the official park map or other maps available online. In any case, the junction marks the end of the hike's most difficult leg, and from here it's a much more forgiving experience.

About 200 feet past the junction, this unnamed trail S-curves to the right and then the left as it proceeds south. You continue to gain elevation, but now it's much more gradual. The trail becomes more defined and the tree cover opens slightly, revealing isolated views of the valley below and open sky overhead. A number of broad, flat spaces alongside the sides of the trail in this section are ideal for picnickers or those just looking to take a load off.

At about 1.25 miles, the trail curves left and then right (southeast). As you come out of the curve, the trail reaches its peak elevation, and almost immediately you begin to descend, gradually at first and then more steeply starting about 0.25 mile later.

The final leg of the trail is marked by numerous twists and switchbacks along its descent. Take care in this home stretch: the Mount Spokane area receives considerably more rainfall than the rest of the region, and the trail can get quite muddy and slick in the spring and fall.

At almost 1.6 miles, you enter a curve to the right, and the most rewarding vistas of the entire hike open to your right (north). The stunning views span the entire mountain valley, with treetops and fog-slashed peaks rising high overhead. Capture a few snapshots and pick some berries, proceeding carefully and with an eye toward trail conditions as necessary.

The final 0.5 mile of the loop is also the wildest. At the 1.9-mile mark, the trail bends sharply to the left (south) and then makes a hairpin turn right (north). (On a map, this part looks sort of like an eagle's beak.) Past the hairpin, the trail makes a hard turn right (east) and then, 0.15 mile later, whips left and then right. Coming out of this S-curve at 2.25 miles, you make a hard left and then a final right near the snow-tubing field. Walk straight across the field to the footbridge, and take it back to the parking lot.

Nearby Attractions

This hike, like many others within the state park trail network, is close to several local eateries, among them **Chaney's Bottoms-Up Inn** (509-238-9188) and, just across the road, **Bear Creek Lodge** (509-238-9114, bearcreeklodgewa.com). Snowmobilers and cross-country skiers also frequent this area in winter, and a number of area wilderness groups plan group snowshoeing excursions (see Appendix C, page 192). Finally, you're just a short drive from the famed **Green Bluff** agricultural area, home to an impressive array of farms, orchards, and meaderies (see greenbluffgrowers.com for more information).

Directions

From Monroe Street in downtown Spokane, take I-90 eastbound. After roughly 7 miles, take Exit 287 left (north) onto North Mullan Road, which becomes North Argonne Road after 0.1 mile and then North Bruce Road 6.1 miles after that. In another 2.3 miles, take the first exit off the traffic circle right (east) onto WA 206/East Mount Spokane Park Drive, which switchbacks generally northeast. (*Note:* Past the traffic circle, cell coverage becomes unreliable to nonexistent.) After about 13 miles, look for a large gravel parking area on your right (Bear Creek Lodge is just ahead on your left).

Northern Idaho

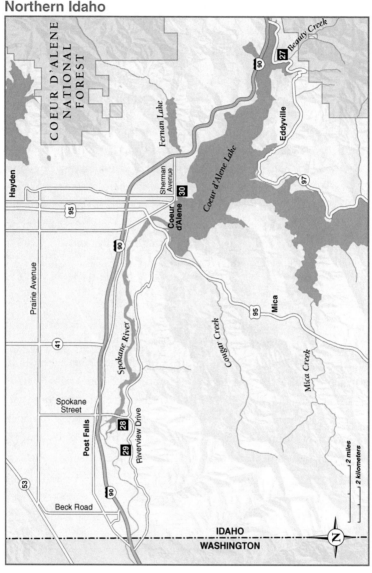

Northern Idaho

COEUR D'ALENE LAKE OVERLOOK, TUBBS HILL (SEE HIKE 30, PAGE 185)

SCENERY: ★ ★ ★ ★ ★
TRAIL CONDITION: ★ ★ ★ ★ ★
CHILDREN: ★ ★ ★ ★
DIFFICULTY: ★ ★
SOLITUDE: ★ ★ ★

UPHILL CLIMB ON THE MINERAL RIDGE NATIONAL RECREATION TRAIL

GPS TRAILHEAD COORDINATES: N47° 36.955' W116° 40.711'

DISTANCE & CONFIGURATION: 3.0-mile loop

HIKING TIME: 1 hour

HIGHLIGHTS: Views of Coeur d'Alene Lake and the surrounding mountains, excellent raptor-watching, cooler summertime temperatures than most of the Spokane area

ELEVATION: 2,160' at lowest point, 2,708' at highest

ACCESS: Daily, 8 a.m.–sunset; no fees or permits. This hike is best in autumn, when bald eagles and ospreys hunt for fish during the annual salmon run.

MAPS: USGS *Mount Coeur d'Alene, ID;* tinyurl.com/mineralridgetrailmap and at trailhead

FACILITIES: Restrooms, covered picnic areas, map board, paved parking, and disability ramp at trailhead

WHEELCHAIR ACCESS: Yes

COMMENTS: Dogs must be leashed; biking, hunting, and horseback riding are prohibited.

CONTACTS: Bureau of Land Management, Coeur d'Alene Field Office, 208-769-5000, blm.gov/visit /mineral-ridge-scenic-area-and-national-recreation-trail

Overview

Located 10 minutes from Coeur d'Alene, this hike is the farthest east in this book but still readily accessible from Spokane. The moderately trafficked trail boasts pristine old-growth conifer forests as well as breathtaking views of Coeur d'Alene Lake and the surrounding valley.

This hike strikes a good balance between easy and challenging. While it's somewhat steeper than many similar hikes, the mostly gentle grades make it a good choice for families. The trail is also surprisingly accessible for visitors in wheelchairs, though they may need some help navigating the rockier portions as well as the final switchback descent. Seniors will want to bring trekking poles for this last stretch.

Route Details

Begin this hike from the parking area. Walk up the disability ramp, noting the relevant contact information on the nearby information board; follow the switchbacks, and then when the trail comes to a fork, turn right (east).

The initial ascent proceeds through dense forests of pine and spruce. The ridge from which the trail and scenic area take their name is bordered on three sides by the blue-green waters of Coeur d'Alene Lake, with steep mountain slopes in all directions. In springtime, the forest floor is blanketed with wild-flowers such as snowdrops, wild orchids, and currants.

The trail is helpfully marked by wooden fences at key intervals—use these as a visual guide to remain on the correct path. Please heed the posted signage and resist the impulse to take shortcuts, which contributes to soil erosion. Interpretive stations along the trail describe the area's natural and human history. Feel free to take breaks as necessary—this hike has an abundance of conveniently placed benches for the weary.

About 250 feet past the initial fork, you come to another switchback—follow it left and then right, at which point the trail begins a gentle ascent. After about 0.5 mile, past two more benches along your left, take the next switchback left. Continue north and west up the trail for about 0.1 mile; then take the next switchback to the right (northeast).

As you continue to ascend, the local underbrush gives way to grassy clearings and evidence of recent controlled burns. According to the notice back at

Mineral Ridge National Recreation Trail

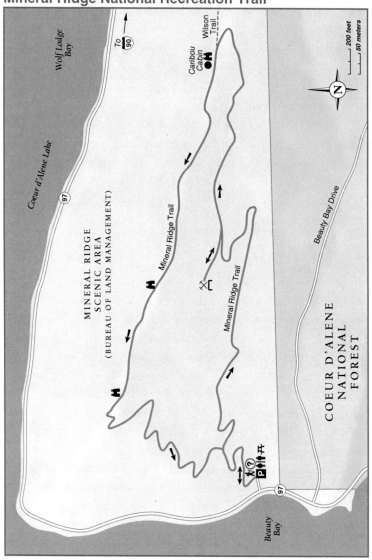

the trailhead, the federal Bureau of Land Management creates planned fires on a regular basis that help clear the area of dry kindling, which also protects larger, older trees. Safety measures aside, bear in mind that campfires, smoking, and fireworks are still banned across much of this region during the summer months, and for good reason.

About 200 feet past the previous switchback, you reach a marked offshoot to the left. This spur and its accompanying sign point to a compelling facet of the region's history, specifically the 19th-century mining rush. Follow this branch off to the left—it's only a few hundred paces and is a straight shot back to the main trail. At the end, along with a small bench, you'll find a large hole, only about 8–12 feet deep, bored straight into the rock face.

According to the signs, when this land was being taken over by settlers, leasing companies were quick to package large tracts for sale as potential mining prospects, hence the name Mineral Ridge. Much of the land turned out to be unusable, however, due to both the nature of the rock and the lack of precious ore deposits that speculators promised. Snap a few photos, being mindful that mountain lions and other wildlife have been known to seek shelter in the abandoned shaft; then return to the main path and continue left (northeast).

In less than 0.5 mile, the trail hooks left (west) and begins its return leg. At this altitude, the heavy tree cover thins a bit. Make sure to get a few shots of the ridgelines facing both north and east. After 50 feet or so, you reach a junction with the Wilson Trail on the right—take the left fork for Caribou Cabin. The trail continues to gain elevation, and you're now past the hike's halfway point.

The views from the top of the ridge are nothing short of stunning. Linger a bit at Caribou Cabin before you resume your westward trek back toward home.

This next portion constitutes the longest and final straightaway. About 0.4 mile past Caribou Cabin, you reach the hike's high point (2,708') and another overlook to your right (north). If you've struggled with the climb so far, you can take a brief sigh of relief as the path now begins to descend, culminating in

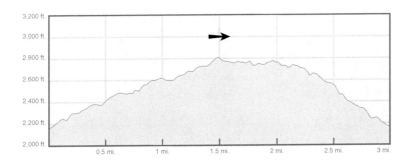

another overlook and rest area at the northwest edge of the ridge, about 0.2 mile past the high point.

Here lies the true payoff of this hike: a breathtaking panorama spanning the whole of Coeur d'Alene Lake, with mountains stretching in all directions. In the fall, bring binoculars to watch the raptors hunting salmon.

A couple of hundred feet past the second overlook, you swing left and begin the final, twisty southbound stretch. Comprising a series of switchbacks, this section becomes much steeper as you descend; follow the sections of trail marked by fenceposts, and again, *avoid making shortcuts.* Trekking poles will come in handy here if you're unsteady on your feet.

At about 2.25 miles, you emerge back at the initial junction to close the loop, with the parking lot visible through the trees down the hill. Turn right at the fork and take it back to the trailhead.

Nearby Attractions

Before you head back to Spokane, consider a detour in **Coeur d'Alene**, just west of this hike. When the weather is warm, you can take a posthike dip at one of the public beaches close to downtown. For upscale cuisine with waterfront views, try **Bardenay** (bardenay.com) or **The Cedars** (cedarsfloatingrestaurant.com). The sprawling **Coeur d'Alene Resort** (cdaresort.com) has luxurious accommodations along with 11 restaurants, a spa, a golf course, and water recreation. If you're looking for something a little more low-key, the **Moose Lounge** (facebook.com /moosecda) and **The Buoy** (thebuoycda.com) are popular watering holes, and **Calypsos** (calypsoscoffee.com) serves some of the best coffee in town.

Directions

From Monroe Street in downtown Spokane, take I-90 eastbound about 41 miles into Idaho; then take Exit 22 for ID 97 toward Harrison, and turn right (south) at the stop sign onto ID 97. After 1.8 miles, turn left (south) to continue on ID 97; the parking lot is 0.4 mile ahead on the left.

Post Falls Community Forest: Q'emlin Park Access

SCENERY: ★ ★ ★ ★ ★
TRAIL CONDITION: ★ ★
CHILDREN: ★ ★ ★
DIFFICULTY: ★ ★ ★ ★
SOLITUDE: ★ ★ ★

RIVER VIEWS ABOUND ALONG THE NORTHERN PART OF THE LOOP.

GPS TRAILHEAD COORDINATES: N47° 42.119' W116° 57.342'

DISTANCE & CONFIGURATION: 2.3-mile balloon

HIKING TIME: 1.15 hours

HIGHLIGHTS: Breathtaking cliffs, dense forest cover, views of the Spokane River

ELEVATION: 2,078' at lowest point, 2,181' at highest

ACCESS: Daily, sunrise–midnight (best March–October). No fees or permits are required to hike, but parking in Q'emlin Park, immediately east of the trailhead, requires a daily pass ($5) or seasonal pass ($15 residents, $30 nonresidents) Memorial Day–Labor Day. Free parking is available on the north side of Parkway Drive just outside the park gates.

MAPS: The official park map (download at the website below) is a must-have on this hike to avoid getting lost—either print it out in color or save it to your phone. The same map is also posted at the trailhead.

FACILITIES: Portable toilet and map board at trailhead

WHEELCHAIR ACCESS: No

COMMENTS: Leashed dogs allowed in Post Falls Community Forest; pets prohibited in Q'emlin Park

CONTACTS: City of Post Falls Department of Parks and Recreation, 208-773-1722, postfallsidaho.org /departments/parks-recreation/parks/community-forest

Post Falls Community Forest: Q'emlin Park Access

Overview

Located in Post Falls, Idaho, just across the state line from Washington, this short loop in Post Falls Community Forest takes visitors through picturesque woods and stunning basalt cliffs a world away from the bustle of Spokane. It visits a scenic viewpoint overlooking the Spokane River and is ideal for solo hikers, pet owners, and families with older kids who have some hiking experience.

Be aware, however, that the trail quality fluctuates wildly, making it easy to get lost amid the rock formations and dense woodland undergrowth. The rugged terrain is also a poor fit for older hikers and those with disabilities.

Something else to consider is the system of color-coded markers throughout the trail network, encompassing both signposts and blazes on trees. Instead of text, these markers consist of circles and diamonds in blue, green, orange, purple, red, and yellow. A particular color–shape combination corresponds to a particular trail—the Green Circle Trail is a 3.7-mile loop, for example, while the Purple Diamond Trail is a 1.9-mile one-way/3.8-mile out-and-back route—but in most cases you'll see multiple markers arranged vertically on a signpost or blaze, indicating that several trails overlap on a given segment.

On one hand, this system enables a wealth of possibilities for creating custom routes; on the other hand, it's easy to get off-course if you don't know what you're doing. So plan ahead and familiarize yourself with the trails. Also bring along a color printout of the official park map (see "Maps," page 172) or download it to your phone; the same map is posted at the trailhead, but that's no substitute for having it with you on the trail.

For this guide, numbers on the trail map (opposite) are keyed to corresponding numbered bullets in the description that follows. **Our trail map is not a replacement for the official map.**

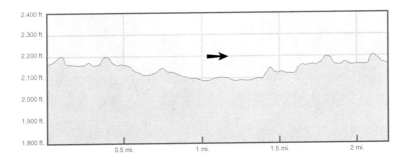

Route Details

This hike begins about a block west of the streetside parking lot on Parkway Drive. With Q'emlin Park on your right and a residential area on your left, walk straight ahead (west) and then take the first right past the parking checkpoint. Then access the trailhead nearest the Post Falls Community Forest entrance on the left, ❶ marked by a map board, portable toilet, and trash can. Trail markers here indicate the Green Circle, Orange Diamond, and Purple Diamond Trails. Continue straight (northwest), and about 200 feet ahead, the Blue Circle Trail merges in from the left. ❷

The trail is rugged from the start, with numerous branches crisscrossing over uneven terrain. The path bears left (south) and passes through a short (350') downhill segment between two rock formations, at which point one of

LOOKING INTO THE GORGE ALONG THE TRAIL'S INITIAL STRETCH

this trail's defining features becomes apparent: a sheer set of cliffs that descend more than 100 hundred feet into a deep woodland gorge. Be sure to get a few photos of the majestic view here. Make note as well of the stone stairs helpfully set into the cliffside, and take considerable care while descending. Trekking poles are highly recommended here.

Once you reach the bottom of the cliffs, thankfully, the rest of the trail is remarkably smooth. ❸ Follow the wide trail uphill and to the right (northwest), taking care to avoid the numerous offshoots that wander off into the brush. This portion of the hike will be long and straight, with several moderate rises and falls. The cliffs loom just overhead to the right and farther across the gorge to the left, providing a striking sense of contrast. Summer hikers, note the numerous species of wildflower just off the path—these make for excellent photo ops.

At a little more than 0.5 mile from the trailhead, you come to a four-way intersection. ❹ To your far right, the Blue Circle Trail heads east. Straight ahead, an unmarked connector trail rises imposingly to the northeast; to your far left, an unnamed spur heads southwest; and finally, to your more immediate left, the Orange Diamond Trail heads west—this is the one you want.

From here, the hike reaches a different phase, descending gradually through deep forests of pine and Douglas-fir. On a clear day, you can make out the Spokane River through the trees—use the river as a reference point if necessary, as it lies due north of your current location.

About 0.1 mile later, you reach another junction: where the Orange Diamond Trail continues left, turn right (northwest) and uphill onto the Yellow Circle Trail, ❺ passing an unmarked connector trail to your right shortly after the junction. Another 0.1 mile later, the trail curves left, continuing generally northwest; then, about 0.2 mile farther, turn right (northeast) on the Green Circle Trail. ❻

The trail bends left, then right, and about 0.1 mile later (the 1-mile mark overall), you arrive at the turnaround point for the loop portion of his hike. ❼ The rightmost path, still the Green Circle Trail, will take you back toward the trailhead, but the left fork—an unmarked out-and-back spur ❽ leading north to the Spokane River—is worth making a detour for. Follow it downhill about 350 feet, and you'll be rewarded with a serene view of the river. Grab a few shots or just chill and take in the peaceful scenery; when you're ready, head back south on the spur to the previous intersection, and turn left (east) on the Green Circle Trail. ❾ About 350 feet later, you reach another trail junction—where the Green Circle Trail continues right (southeast), bear left (east) onto the Purple Circle Trail. ❿

The trail follows the river for a bit, curving left and then right as it moves from west to east. Then, about 0.15 mile from the previous junction, you reach another spur trail branching off to the left (northeast). ⓫ Follow this a few yards to a small, grassy spit of land overlooking the river, across from which is the redbrick bulk of the city's hydroelectric plant. This is a lovely spot for a picnic lunch, as the ground here is generally flat and dry, but heed the signs warning visitors away from the water (the Post Falls Dam lies just downstream to the southeast), which can be extremely dangerous for swimmers. When ready, return on the spur to the Purple Circle Trail, and turn left to follow it south. ⓬ This next segment becomes more uneven, with hidden rocks and tree roots to catch the unwary traveler. Expect a few up-and-down portions through here.

Just shy of the 1.5-mile mark, the Purple Circle Trail swings right (northeast), and in 100 feet or so, you reach yet another fork—where the combined Purple Circle/Green Circle Trail bears left (southwest), go right, now back on the Green Circle Trail. ⓭ About 260 feet farther, you reach still another fork—where the Green Circle Trail continues straight into the gorge, amid denser underbrush, you turn left to go southwest on the other, less visible path, ⓮ an unnamed connector that leads up a series of rocky escarpments. Take care while climbing, and be mindful of your footing.

About 160 feet later, the trail bends left (southeast) and begins a descent of about 0.2 mile. The path here is narrow, with dense vegetation on all sides—inspect yourself for ticks at the end of the hike. At a little more than 1.7 miles from the trailhead, you reach the four-way intersection where you began the loop. Continue straight ahead (southeast), now on the combined Blue Circle/Orange Diamond Trail. ⓯

Past the intersection, the path resumes its upward course and then descends again about 0.1 mile farther; before long, you're once again in the shadow of the cliffs from earlier. Take care here, as this section is popular with climbing enthusiasts, and both trail condition and definition deteriorate. Owing to the rugged terrain, you can deviate by even a few yards, as I did, and find yourself in radically unfamiliar territory. Maintain a generally easterly course, take regular pauses to reorient, and stay alert for the diamond-shaped blue and orange markers, and you should be able to find your way.

At around the 2-mile mark, or about 0.35 mile past where you closed the loop, the combined Green Circle/Purple Diamond Trail merges in from the right. ⑯ A couple of hundred feet later, you arrive back at the bottom of the cliffs from the trail's outset—ascend the stairs with care, and then proceed on the final uphill (southeast) stretch to the trailhead. ⑰ As you near the end of the hike, you should see the Q'emlin Park parking area off to the left (north). At about the 2.2-mile mark, where the Blue Circle Trail heads left, ⑱ keep right (southeast) and walk the last 365 feet or so downhill to exit at the parking checkpoint and, with any luck, not far from your car. ⑲

Nearby Attractions

See the next hike for a trek that starts at the community forest's southern trailhead, just off West Riverview Drive. Post Falls makes for a lovely escape from the bustle of Spokane, with great scenery and an abundance of public parks. Take a dip in the designated swimming areas at **Q'Emlin Park,** just east of this hike, or head into town and check out the numerous dining options on offer. **Coeur d'Alene** is just a few minutes' drive to the east, while to the west, just across the Washington border, lies **Liberty Lake.** Both towns offer a wealth of recreational options, making this hike the perfect starting point for any number of fun family excursions.

Directions

From Monroe Street in downtown Spokane, take I-90 eastbound, entering Idaho after about 20 miles. About 3.5 miles farther, take Exit 5 toward Spokane Street/City Center in Post Falls; then turn right (south) onto North Spokane Street, and drive 0.7 mile. Just after you cross the Spokane River, take the first right onto West Parkway Drive. Free parking is available in the lot along the right (north) side of the street; if this lot is full, additional parking is available in Q'emlin Park, around the corner and to the right (a parking fee is charged Memorial Day–Labor Day).

29 Post Falls Community Forest: Riverview Drive Access

SCENERY: ★ ★ ★ ★ ★
TRAIL CONDITION: ★ ★ ★
CHILDREN: ★ ★ ★
DIFFICULTY: ★ ★ ★
SOLITUDE: ★ ★ ★ ★

MUDDY TRACKS MARK THE TRAIL AFTER A SPRING RAIN.

GPS TRAILHEAD COORDINATES: N47° 41.786' W116° 58.375'

DISTANCE & CONFIGURATION: 2.9-mile balloon

HIKING TIME: 1.25 hours

HIGHLIGHTS: Dense and secluded forest hiking, stellar views of the Spokane River

ELEVATION: 2,071' at lowest point, 2,447' at highest

ACCESS: Daily, sunrise–sunset (best March–October); no fees or permits

MAPS: The official park map (download at the website below) is a must-have on this hike to avoid getting lost—either print it out in color or save it to your phone. The same map is also posted at the trailhead.

FACILITIES: Restrooms, map board, and parking at trailhead

WHEELCHAIR ACCESS: No

COMMENTS: Dogs must be leashed

CONTACTS: City of Post Falls Department of Parks and Recreation, 208-773-1722, postfallsidaho.org /departments/parks-recreation/parks/community-forest

Overview

Consisting largely of unpaved footpaths through secluded woodlands, following the banks of the Spokane River, this hike is suited both to older hikers and families. Like the previous hike, it makes use of the rather complex color-coded trail network within Post Falls Community Forest, so plan ahead and familiarize yourself with the trails. Also bring along a color printout of the official park map (see "Maps," opposite) or download it to your phone; the same map is posted at the trailhead, but that's no substitute for having it with you on the trail.

For this guide, numbers on the trail map (see next page) are keyed to corresponding numbered bullets in the description that follows. **Our trail map is not a replacement for the official map.**

Route Details

Begin from the paved parking area just north of West Riverview Drive. **❶** Review the posted signage before proceeding past the service gate. The initial leg consists of a wooded straightaway proceeding left (west-northwest) from the trailhead for a little more than 0.3 mile, passing a junction to your right just a couple hundred feet along the way. Markers for this segment indicate the Purple Circle, Yellow Circle, Blue Diamond, Orange Diamond, and Red Circle Trails.

As you hike, pay attention to the local flora and fauna. The climate here is cooler and damper than it is around Spokane, providing a fertile environment for dense forest cover. Ponderosa and lodgepole pines abound here as they do back west, though in northern Idaho it's not uncommon to see the trunks and branches draped in moss. Dress for the weather, as strong breezes and rain are especially common here in spring.

When the trail forks, veer sharply to the right onto the combined Orange Diamond/Red Circle Trail. **❷** The next section is a bit more winding, heading downhill north and east before descending into a series of switchbacks. Note the purple wildflowers lining the sides of the path—this is wild currant, which come August yields a profusion of berries ripe for eating straight off the vine. Springtime visitors will find an abundance of blooms among the undergrowth, including yellow daisy, hyacinth, and the ubiquitous snowdrop.

About 0.2 mile past the fork marking the beginning of the loop, follow the first hairpin curve to the left; then, a few hundred yards down, double back to

Post Falls Community Forest: Riverview Drive Access

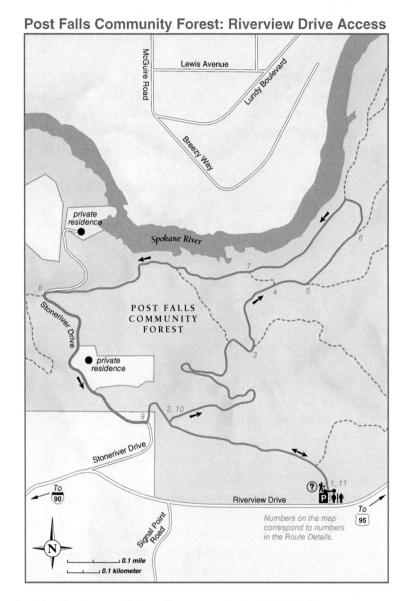

McGuire Road

Lewis Avenue

Lundy Boulevard

Breezy Way

private residence

Spokane River

8

Stoneriver Drive

6

7

POST FALLS COMMUNITY FOREST

4

5

private residence

3

9

2, 10

Stoneriver Drive

To
90

Signal Point Road

Riverview Drive

1, 11

To
95

Numbers on the map correspond to numbers in the Route Details.

N

0.1 mile
0.1 kilometer

the right. Don't worry if the trail appears to be headed back the way you came—as long as you continue to descend, you should be fine.

At 0.9 mile an unmarked trail heads northwest, but you continue straight, heading briefly northeast, then southeast. In just a few hundred feet, you reach another fork—bear left (north) onto the combined Green Circle/Orange Diamond Trail. ❸ In about 0.1 mile, the path gradually curves right (east) and then intersects an east–west trail. ❹ Left (west) is the combined Blue Diamond/Orange Diamond Trail; right (east) is the combined Green Circle/Yellow Circle/Blue Diamond/Orange Diamond Trail—go right.

In about 370 feet, you reach another fork—where the Blue Diamond/Orange Diamond Trail continues right (east), you bear left onto the Green Circle/Yellow Circle Trail, now on a straightaway heading northeast. ❺ At 1.3 miles, the path curves left, heading in a more northerly direction onto an unmarked connector trail; then, a little more than 200 feet past that, you continue left (southwest) onto the Purple Circle Trail. ❻ At this point you should have a clear view of the river.

This close to the falls, high stands of pine and fir hem the river in on both banks. The waters move high and fast, particularly in springtime, so use caution as you navigate the rocks along the southern bank. This portion of the river is blocked downstream by a sizable hydroelectric dam, making it unsuitable for both swimmers and kayakers.

At a little more than 1.5 miles from the trailhead, the route gradually curves right (west) and straightens; about 0.1 mile farther, the Blue Diamond/Orange Diamond Trail merges in from the left. ❼ This westbound section has some slight ups and downs but is generally well kept and easy to follow. It's also both the most scenic and the longest straightaway of the hike, coming in at roughly 0.3 mile. Summertime hikers, be mindful of blackflies this close to the water. Insect repellent and long trousers are advised in all seasons.

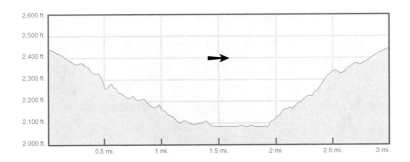

Just past the 1.8-mile mark, the trail begins to rise again as it bends to the west. You now climb back through dense woodlands marked by dramatic rocky outcrops, which are ideal for climbing enthusiasts. The less adventurous should nevertheless snap a few photos, as the views here are lovely. Then, 0.2 mile ahead, the dirt trail meets South Stoneriver Drive, a paved residential street—follow Stoneriver as it makes a hairpin turn back to the left (southeast). **8**

The paved section, not quite 0.3 mile long, passes a private home on your left about halfway along; note that in this stretch, the park map designates Stoneriver Drive as the combined Blue Diamond/Purple Circle/Yellow Circle Trail, though there are no markers. Then, at a little more than 2.4 miles, you reach another fork. **9** Where Stoneriver Drive veers right and continues south, turn sharply left (north) back onto a dirt trail, and follow it as it curves just as sharply to the right (south), using the fences to your right as a guide. (Like the paved stretch before it, this segment is marked as the Blue Diamond/Purple Circle/Yellow Circle Trail.)

About 0.1 mile after leaving the paved road, you arrive back at the original fork to close the balloon. **10** Where the Orange Diamond/Red Circle Trail heads left, bear right (southeast) and climb the final 0.4 mile to the trailhead. **11**

Nearby Attractions

With its river access, numerous parks, and sense of small-town charm, Post Falls makes for a refreshing summertime getaway. If you're hungry after your hike, swing by **Capone's Pub and Grill** (caponespub.com/post-falls) or **Post Falls Brewing Company** (postfallsbrewing.com). Or treat yourself to a picnic at **Falls Park,** about 2.5 miles north across the Spokane River, or **Q'emiln Park,** adjacent to Post Falls Community Forest's eastern trailhead (see previous hike).

Directions

From Monroe Street in downtown Spokane, take I-90 eastbound for about 19 miles; then take Exit 299 and turn right (south) onto Spokane Bridge Road. In 0.4 mile, bear left at the fork onto West Riverview Drive, and enter Idaho about 0.1 mile farther. Continue east on West Riverview Drive about 3.7 miles; the trailhead parking area will be on your left.

YOU'LL CROSS THIS ROPE BRIDGE ON THE EAST SIDE OF THE LOOP.

SCENERY: ★ ★ ★ ★ ★
TRAIL CONDITION: ★ ★ ★ ★
CHILDREN: ★ ★ ★
DIFFICULTY: ★ ★
SOLITUDE: ★ ★

GPS TRAILHEAD COORDINATES: N47° 40.229' W116° 46.913'

DISTANCE & CONFIGURATION: 2.5-mile loop

HIKING TIME: 1 hour

HIGHLIGHTS: Views of Lake Coeur d'Alene, excellent bird-watching

ELEVATION: 2,139' at lowest point, 2,340' at highest

ACCESS: Daily, 8 a.m.–sunset. No fees or permits are required to hike, but you must pay to park inside McEuen Park, through which you must walk to access the trailhead at Tubbs Hill ($1/hour or $2/hour depending on location). Two-hour free parking is available on the north side of Front Avenue, just north of the park. For an interactive map showing additional parking spots nearby, see maps.cdaid.org/parking.

MAPS: USGS *Coeur d'Alene, ID*; downloadable and interactive maps at maps.cdaid.org/tubbs and tubbshill.org/maps

FACILITIES: Restrooms, signage, trash cans, and restaurant at western trailhead

WHEELCHAIR ACCESS: No

COMMENTS: Dogs must be leashed

CONTACTS: City of Coeur d'Alene Parks and Recreation Department, 208-769-2300, cdaid.org/tubbs-hill; Friends of Tubbs Hill, tubbshill.org

Tubbs Hill: Main Trail

Numbers indicate interpretive trail markers.

P — McEUEN PARK

Military Memorial

The Buoy

1 27 26 25

Tubbs Hill Drive

24

23

Main Trail

22

21

20

TUBBS HILL

Summit Trail

water tank

swinging bridge

Tubbs Hill

water tank

19

18

17

16

15

Main Trail

6 7

8

Tubbs Hill Beach

Main Trail

9

10

11

12 13

14

(official turnaround)

2

3

4

5

Lakeside Avenue

6th Street 7th Street 9th Street

To 90

Sherman Avenue

2nd Street 4th Street 5th Street

Front Avenue

10th Street

Mullan Avenue

8th Street

Bancroft Avenue

11th Street

Young Avenue

Pine Avenue

Mountain Avenue

10th Street

East Tubbs Trail

To 90

N

0.1 mile

0.1 kilometer

Coeur D'Alene Lake

Overview

In the thriving heart of downtown Coeur d'Alene just south of McEuen Park, Tubbs Hill is a well-known landmark popular with both locals and tourists alike. Set on 120 acres of public land, this natural area overlooks the shores of Coeur d'Alene Lake and affords awe-inspiring views of the water and the surrounding mountains. The moderately trafficked Main Trail, which circles the perimeter of the park, has mostly modest altitude gains and is great for families with older kids and pets.

Route Details

From the west side of the parking lot in McEuen Park, at the southwest corner of East Front Avenue and South Third Street, look for a paved path leading left and then south alongside Third Street. About 350 feet from the parking lot, continue straight (south) along the western edge of the Military Memorial plaza, with Coeur d'Alene Lake to your right. About 300 feet farther, turn left in front of The Buoy restaurant; then turn right (south) on the sidewalk and go around to the back of the building, where the paved path ends and Tubbs Hill's Main Trail begins.

The trailhead is marked by a moose sculpture on the right, along with rocks and signs on both sides of the trail indicating the day's fire risk and other relevant information. Head straight (south) on the dirt path.

The Main Trail rises sharply from the outset, over a series of basalt outcrops blanketed by moss. About 180 feet from the trailhead, you come to a junction with a sign for trail marker 1 on a tree to your left (east); pay attention to these interpretive markers, of which there are 27 in all along the trail (see map opposite). Bear right (south) at the fork to stay on the main path.

The initial leg winds generally south, passing a junction with a fire road to your left about 380 feet from the previous fork. Steep embankments lie just off

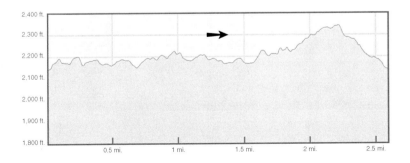

to your right—older hikers, or those who are less sure in their footing, will want to bring trekking poles, but thankfully the trail itself is well kept. About 0.4 mile ahead, you pass another fire-road junction to your left; then, about 260 feet past that, the trail swings left (east); just past the turnoff is the first of several scenic overlooks, this one just above Tubbs Hill Beach. Take some time here to snap a few photos, as this area offers some of the most picturesque views in the region. Those making the journey in the fall may even have a chance to spy bald eagles and ospreys, hunting salmon as the fish make their seasonal run inland to spawn.

Now heading east, the Main Trail curves right about 0.1 mile past the overlook, then left again after another 0.1 mile. By this point, you're heading due south; continue to be mindful of the cliffs.

The scenery in this stretch is absolutely stunning, especially on a clear day. Note the diversity of plant life along the trail—in springtime you'll be treated to wildflowers such as yellow orchids, purple wood violets, and white snowdrops. The ground cover is mostly a combination of lichens and moss, a far departure from the dry grasses and sage of the West Plains back in Washington. And in addition to the ponderosa pines common to the Spokane area, you'll spot spruces and firs as well as the occasional cedar.

After about 0.25 mile on the southbound stretch, the trail hooks to the left (east). About 0.1 mile farther, just past a junction to your left with the Summit Trail (which leads north to the top of Tubbs Hill), you'll come to trail marker 13, noted by the signs as the official turnaround for this hike. Continue over the rise another 0.1 mile, past a spur to the lakeshore on your right and another fire-road junction to your left, as the Main Trail now begins to wind its way left (north).

About 0.1 mile from the previous turnoff, the path begins to diverge inland and away from the lake. Look to your right (east) for views of the southern marina and a few sleepy residential areas. Off to the north, the views only become more striking, with the Coeur d'Alene skyline above the treetops, framed against the mountains beyond.

In another 0.25 mile, you come to a small swinging bridge—dog owners will want to divert down the small draw to the left, as the wooden slats can be difficult for small paws to manage. About 0.1 mile past the bridge, the route ascends a set of small stone stairs, after which you arrive at another fork in the trail. Per the posted signage, going left takes you back to McEuen Park, while right will take you to 10th Street—for this hike, take the left fork. Pass another fire-road junction to your right another 100 feet ahead.

Past these junctions, the elevation rises sharply and the tree cover grows much more dense. In another 0.3 mile, just past the trail's high point, the trail forks yet again, where it meets the Summit Trail again—go right and cross Tubbs Hill Drive.

The final 0.2-mile leg now descends north, northwest, and then due west through dense forest on a series of switchbacks. Be mindful of the terrain, as the path is rocky and uneven, and several trouble spots present fall risks. Fortunately, this section is brief and easily navigated, provided you proceed slowly and carefully. After about 2 miles of hiking, you once again pass trail marker 1 to close the loop. Bear right at the fork to return to the trailhead and the parking lot beyond.

Nearby Attractions

Given its location in the heart of downtown Coeur d'Alene and its proximity to the lakeshore, this hike has numerous attractions to recommend it. Linger on the public greens of **McEuen Park**, perhaps with a picnic lunch, or head south to **Tubbs Hill Beach** for a swim and a little sun. From here, you can wander next door to the **Coeur d'Alene Resort** (cdaresort.com) to check out its many dining and recreational options. For something a little more homey, not to mention closer in, **The Buoy** (thebuoycda.com)—right next to the trailhead for this hike—is another local favorite, serving burgers, sandwiches, tacos, craft beer, and frozen cocktails.

Directions

From Monroe Street in downtown Spokane, take I-90 eastbound, entering Idaho after about 20 miles; then, about 10 miles farther, take Exit 11 right (south) onto Northwest Boulevard in Coeur d'Alene. In 2 miles, bear left (east) as Northwest becomes East Sherman Avenue; then, in 0.1 mile (two blocks), turn right (south) onto North Third Street and take the first left onto East Front Avenue. Then either bear left into the McEuen Park parking lot just across Front Avenue (fee applies) or continue east on Front and park in the free lot along the left (north) side of the street. The trailhead is just east of The Buoy restaurant, at the southwest edge of McEuen Park.

Appendix A:
Outdoor Retailers

BIG 5 SPORTING GOODS
7501 N. Division St.
Spokane, WA 99208
509-467-6970
tinyurl.com/big5washingtonstores

DICK'S SPORTING GOODS
14014 E. Indiana Ave.
Spokane Valley, WA 99216
509-891-0977
tinyurl.com/dicksspokanevalley

THE NORTH FACE
714 W. Main St.
Spokane, WA 99201
509-747-5389
stores.thenorthface.com/wa/spokane/usa47

NORTHWEST OUTDOORS
3220 N. Division St.
Spokane, WA 99207
509-327-2050
nwoutdoors.co

REI
1125 N. Monroe St.
Spokane, WA 99201
509-328-9000
rei.com/stores/spokane

SPORTSMAN'S WAREHOUSE
6720 N. Division St.
Spokane, WA 99208
509-487-0700
tinyurl.com/swspokane

Appendix B:
Map Sources

(Also see **REI** and **Sportsman's Warehouse** on the previous page.)

CITY OF POST FALLS, IDAHO
visitpostfalls.org/maps-guides

CITY OF SPOKANE, WASHINGTON
maps.spokanecity.org

KOOTENAI COUNTY, IDAHO, GEOGRAPHIC INFORMATION SYSTEMS
kcgov.us/178/gis-mapping

SPOKANE COUNTY, WASHINGTON, GEOGRAPHIC INFORMATION SYSTEMS
spokanecounty.org/222/geographic-information-systems

U.S. GEOLOGICAL SURVEY
usgs.gov/products/maps/overview

NEAR THE HIGH POINT OF THE KNOTHEAD VALLEY LOOP, LOOKING EAST
(SEE HIKE 7, PAGE 54)

Appendix C:
Hiking Clubs

HOBNAILERS, INC.

509-487-7366

inlandnorthwesttrails.org/events/hobnailers.asp

INLAND NORTHWEST HIKERS MEETUP GROUP

meetup.com/inland-northwest-hikers

NORTH IDAHO ADVENTURERS CLUB MEETUP GROUP

meetup.com/adventurers-327

SPOKANE MOUNTAINEERS

509-838-4974

spokanemountaineers.org

Index

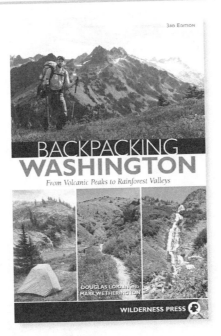

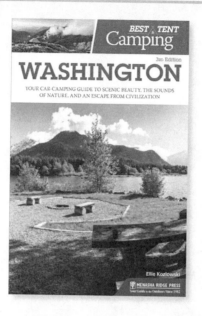

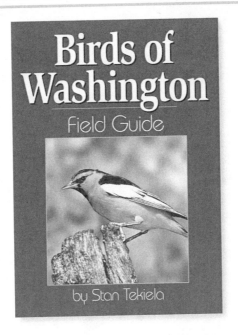

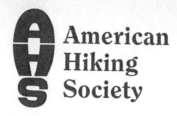

American Hiking Society

PROTECT THE PLACES YOU LOVE TO HIKE.

Become a member today and
take $5 off using the code **Hike5**.

AmericanHiking.org/join

Karl Magnuson / kmagnuson.com

American Hiking Society is the only
national nonprofit organization dedicated
to empowering all to enjoy, share, and
preserve the hiking experience.

DEAR CUSTOMERS AND FRIENDS,

SUPPORTING YOUR INTEREST IN OUTDOOR ADVENTURE, travel, and an active lifestyle is central to our operations, from the authors we choose to the locations we detail to the way we design our books. Menasha Ridge Press was incorporated in 1982 by a group of veteran outdoorsmen and professional outfitters. For many years now, we've specialized in creating books that benefit the outdoors enthusiast.

Almost immediately, Menasha Ridge Press earned a reputation for revolutionizing outdoors- and travel-guidebook publishing. For such activities as canoeing, kayaking, hiking, backpacking, and mountain biking, we established new standards of quality that transformed the whole genre, resulting in outdoor-recreation guides of great sophistication and solid content. Menasha Ridge Press continues to be outdoor publishing's greatest innovator.

The folks at Menasha Ridge Press are as at home on a whitewater river or mountain trail as they are editing a manuscript. The books we build for you are the best they can be, because we're responding to your needs. Plus, we use and depend on them ourselves.

We look forward to seeing you on the river or the trail. If you'd like to contact us directly, visit us at menasharidge.com. We thank you for your interest in our books and the natural world around us all.

SAFE TRAVELS,

Bob Sehlinger

BOB SEHLINGER
PUBLISHER

About the Author

photographed by Micaiah Tinnell

SETH MARLIN is an award-winning, internationally published writer, activist, educator, and poet. A veteran of the Iraq War, he wrote the critically acclaimed blog *The Calm Before the Sand* under a pseudonym from 2006 to 2008. He is also the author of *Shred*, a chapbook of slam poetry, and his prose works have appeared in such publications as *Bark, The Fiction Desk, Knockout, Newfound, Railtown Almanac, RiverLit, Spark, Silk Road Review,* and *Syntax & Salt.* His short story "A Practical Guide to the Resurrected" won the 2016 University of Glasgow Prize for Science Fiction and the Medical Humanities, and his novella "Vigil" was serialized by speculative-fiction magazine *The Colored Lens* in early 2020. He holds a master of fine arts in creative writing from Eastern Washington University.

In his spare time, Seth is a passionate camper and outdoors enthusiast, and for the last decade he has made his home in Spokane with his children.

CPSIA information can be obtained
at www.ICGtesting.com
Printed in the USA
JSRC020603180421
R10806000001B/R108060PG13646JSX00001B/1

9 781634 041348